The Full Rudy

Also by Jack Newfield:

A Prophetic Minority

Robert Kennedy, A Memoir

A Populist Manifesto
(with Jeff Greenfield)

Bread and Roses, Too

Cruel and Unusual Justice

The Permanent Government (with Paul DuBrul)

City for Sale (with Wayne Barrett)

Only in America:
The Life and Crimes of Don King

Somebody's Gotta Tell It: The Upbeat
Memoirs of a Working-Class Journalist

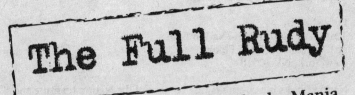

The Full Rudy

The Man, the Myth, the Mania

Jack Newfield

THUNDER'S MOUTH PRESS / NATION BOOKS
NEW YORK

THE FULL RUDY: *The Man, the Myth, the Mania*

Copyright © 2002 Jack Newfield

Published by
Thunder's Mouth Press/Nation Books
161 William St., 16th Floor
New York, NY 10038

Nation Books is a co-publishing venture of the Nation Institute and
Avalon Publishing Group Incorporated.

Library of Congress Cataloging-in-Publication Data is available.

ISBN 1-56025-482-3

9 8 7 6 5 4 3 2 1

Book design by Michael Walters
Printed in the United States of America
Distributed by Publishers Group West

Table Of Contents

"Show me a hero and I will write you a tragedy."

—F. Scott Fitzgerald

For all the victims and heroes of 9/11.

And to my son, Joey, who was there on 9/11, taking pictures like a professional, and who was lucky to survive.

The Full Rudy

1.
The Real Rudy:
The Man and the Myth

The greatest enemy of the truth is very often not the lie—deliberate, contrived and dishonest—but the myth—persistent, persuasive, and unrealistic.

—John F. Kennedy

Rudy Giuliani was a C-plus mayor of New York who has become an A-plus myth in the world.

Since the atrocity of 9/11, Giuliani has artfully merged himself with the wounded city until the man, the metropolis, and this almost religious calamity, seem to be one heroic blur. Ground Zero has become a shrine, and Giuliani its saint.

The funeral pyre for almost 3,000 people has become Giuliani's equivalent of Lincoln's log cabin, or JFK's torpedoed PT-109. This act of mass murder created a new fervent American patriotism that has become the wings of the Giuliani myth.

Giuliani seized ownership of the atrocity, and the camera made him seem like a great man, like Lincoln or

Churchill. But there is something bogus going on here. There is a selective focus. One day has become a career.

The brutal truth is that 9/11 salvaged Giuliani's reputation and career after it had bottomed in 2000. He was facing term limits, and had backed out of a Senate campaign against Hillary Clinton. He was not popular in New York in the months leading up to September 2001.

The purpose of this book is to restore the balance between Giuliani's present image and his complete record, to provide the local detail, context, proportion, and memory.

Giuliani's dark side has not had its national close-up. His national—and international—myth is mostly post–9/11. He has made himself our national grief counselor, patriotic cheerleader, and management guru—while collecting almost $9 million a year in speaking fees.

But please do not misunderstand—or simplify—my point of view. New York did become a better place to live, in many ways, under Giuliani—especially during his first term. Crime went down dramatically. The quality of life improved. Welfare was cut in half. The city's confidence in itself was reinvigorated. His leadership put a strut in the city's step. He banished the feeling that things were out of control.

He had a successful first term from 1994 to 1997, when he was moderate, fresh, focused, not thinking about running statewide for the Senate and not intoxicated by hubris.

But by April 1999, the Quinipiac College Poll showed Giuliani's approval rating among New York City voters down to *40 percent*. It had been *74 percent* fourteen months earlier in the same poll. The main factor in the mayor's drop in popularity was the police killing of unarmed African immigrant Amadou Diallo. More than 60 percent of the city was unhappy with the loss of individual rights, and 82 percent felt that police brutality was "a serious, or somewhat serious," problem in the city. A majority felt that the schools and housing had not improved under Giuliani. During Giuliani's term, only about 75,000 units of new housing were built; during the 1960s, when Robert Wagner and John Lindsay were mayors, 360,000 new units were built.

In the spring of 2000, Giuliani's popularity again slipped below 50 percent, partly as a result of his notifying the media he was separating from his second wife before he bothered to inform his wife. He started appearing in public with Judi Nathan, his mistress. And Raoul Felder, his divorce lawyer, called the mayor's wife, Donna Hanover, an "uncaring mother"—on Mother's Day! Giuliani's popularity also suffered from his attacks on Patrick Dorismond, who had been killed by the police for no reason.

So, well before 9/11, the bloom was off Rudy's rose. He had worn out his welcome with his frequent personal attacks on anyone he didn't like: blacks, black leaders, the homeless, victims of police brutality, free-speech and civil-liberties advocates, AIDS activists, schoolteachers, schools chancellors, taxi drivers, community gardeners, museum artists, sidewalk artists—even singer Billy Joel.

The attack on Billy Joel, now long forgotten, helped open my eyes to the extent of Giuliani's intemperate opportunism.

In February 2000, Hillary Clinton announced her candidacy for the Senate. Before the press conference even began, as reporters and supporters were filing into the room, some low-level campaign aide played a musical tape that included Billy Joel's song, "Captain Jack." (Full disclosure: I'm a big Billy Joel fan.)

The next day at City Hall, Giuliani attacked Clinton for playing a song he called "pro-drug and pro-masturbation."

"Captain Jack," is, in fact, one of the best *anti*-drug anthems ever written. It depicts the life of a drug abuser as empty, lost, and pathetic. It tells the story of a stoner who is all alone on a Saturday night, feeling miserable, and how his mother still has to make his bed although he is twenty-one.

Giuliani distorted the intent of the song to score a cheap political point against the Democrat he thought he was running against for the Senate.

Giuliani's administration lost twenty-seven out of thirty-one lawsuits litigated by the New York Civil Liberties Union (NYCLU) involving violations of the First Amendment.

Giuliani had been a self-described "First Amendment lawyer" in private practice, representing the *Daily News*. But as mayor, he rode roughshod over individual rights, repeatedly trying to curb freedom of speech and freedom of assembly.

Since I had heard him express his "reverence" for the Bill of Rights in private conversations, I asked one of his oldest friends and advisers to explain his new attraction to censorship and repression. This person said, "I can't really explain it. Rudy just has to prove every day that he has the biggest dick in the city, that it's his way or the highway in every situation."

Moreover, during Giuliani's two terms as mayor, the economic disparity between the rich and the poor in New York City grew much wider.

These are all reasons why he needs to be judged over eight years, not just the 112 days between 9/11 and the end of his term in office.

Giuliani has now become a cartoon superhero, based on his performance on 9/11, in front of the cameras. But he was mayor from 1994 through 2001. We should see him the way he was on September 10, which is so-so, and struggling with failing schools, deep racial divisions of his creation, and a huge budget deficit, despite a huge surplus eighteen months earlier.

All politicians want the voters (and the media) to only see the positive side of their character, and not see what they do in the dark, or what they have hidden in their pockets or clenched fists. Rudy Giuliani was more aggressive than most in trying to manage the news and pressure the press.

During the 1990s, when Giuliani was mayor, I was a liberal columnist on the pro-Giuliani *New York Post*. Giuliani, or his communications director, Christine Lategano, would frequently call the paper's editors to micromanage the placement of stories, the tone of headlines, the nuances of captions. They would call after the first edition—and again after the second edition, if all the changes had not been made to their satisfaction.

In May 2002, HBO aired a documentary focused on Giuliani's performance on 9/11. The mayor pitched the project to the cable network himself, actually marketing his own mythmaking. His agent, Brad Grey, was also the co-producer of the special.

A public figure's reputation is the sum of all opinions. It has no objective or scientific basis of its own. A reputation is just the aggregate residue of hype, money, truth, interviews, rumors, journalism, biography, market research, and public relations.

Rudy Giuliani's inflated reputation is the subject of this book, along with his tumultuously mixed performance as mayor of New York.

My purpose is to better synchronize reputation and reality. I hope to offer an objective correlative, before all the hype leads the herd to make Giuliani the vice president, or a cabinet officer, based on a manufactured illusion.

I will emphasize the negatives because these blemishes have lost their proper portion in the big picture. Everyone else seems to be exaggerating the positives.

We should honor what Giuliani did on his best day, but not forget what he did on all his other days. We should remember the day a leader rose to the occasion, but also keep in mind the days when he lowered himself in anger or intolerance.

Giuliani impressed us all by what he did on September 11 (and in the days after), but part of the dazzling was how weak other leaders were.

In the first hours, President Bush was casual and inarticulate. It wasn't until he was given scripted speeches that he appeared presidential. Govenor George Pataki deferred to Giuliani, seeming content to stand behind the take-charge mayor, and look grave.

Giuliani was good, but some of the present mythology comes from the contrast with other politicians who shrank from leadership that first dark day of shock. And some of the mythology comes from the fact *we* need a hero. And Rudy is the closest thing to it. But 9/11 is not about Rudy Giuliani. It is about 2,800 dead. It is about widows, orphans, cops, firefighters, and rescue workers.

In this Age of Media, memory plays tricks on us all. A few videotape highlights, replayed in an endless loop, can replace memory and alter judgment.

The reputations of public figures rise, and fall, and sometimes rise again, over decades. They are constantly being reinvented and reinterpreted by biographers, historians, critics, and documentary filmmakers.

Clark Clifford, for example, started his career in Washington in the 1940s with the image of a fixer. Then he became a "statesman," and then he became a fixer again, when he was indicted in his eighties.

I can remember how reviled Muhammad Ali was in the

1960s, when he was being labeled a "draft dodger" and a "traitor" because of his refusal to fight in Vietnam. Without any due process, he was stripped of his championship by every hack-filled boxing commission in the nation. Then the Supreme Court ruled unanimously that his draft resistance had been legitimately based on his religious faith, and his conviction was overturned.

Now Ali is one of the most beloved persons on the planet—an American Buddha of tragic sweetness. History caught up to him and vindicated him.

Just look at the changing reputations of America's most popular musical performers. Frank Sinatra survived several scandals and cycles of rejection, and then mounted remarkable comebacks. His soulful, swinging voice and exquisite selection of songs prevailed over adversity and fashions. Sinatra could almost always make you *feel something*.

Louis Armstrong was heralded as a jazz genius in the 1920s for his solos, then written off as a "has-been, Uncle Tom" in the 1960s, and then recognized as a genius again—and loved by millions—before he died in 1971. "Pops" has outlasted bebop, doo-wop, and hip-hop.

When Bob Marley died in 1981, this spiritual reggae Rastaman was a superstar only in his native Jamaica, but not in the United States or Europe. But since his passing, his reputation has grown into immortality as new generations discovered his universal music. The man became a myth posthumously on the merits. Marley's "Legends" CD has been the best-selling CD in the world for ten years, among all races and generations. He has become a huge cultural influence and T-shirt icon from rural Africa to the American suburbs.

Alive, Marley was mostly a fringe cult figure among hip musical gourmets. Now he is an international hero of artistic freedom, political rebellion, and musical originality.

For years, Robert Moses had a glorious mythical reputation as the altruistic visionary "master builder" of New York's highways and parks, and as the architect of new housing and "slum clearance." Then one book by Robert Caro changed all that. Caro added the price paid—the dark side left out of the rosy picture. He showed the destruction of organic neighborhoods, the authoritarian decision-making, the insensitivity to blacks, the clubhouse patronage. With one Pulitzer Prize–winning book, Caro authored a new conventional wisdom that has since been incorporated into documentary films and New York histories. Robert Moses is now seen in a totally different light.

I was able to study the discrepancy between reputation and reality in an intimate fashion in 1966 when I began working on a book about Robert Kennedy, which was published after his assassination.

Most of the writing about Robert Kennedy before his assassination contributed to an impression of a "ruthless" and intolerant brute. But the RFK I got to know well, during the last two years of his life, was becoming the exact opposite. He was the most sensitive and compassionate politician I ever saw, when it came to poor people, or children, or anyone who was hurting in some way. He was capable of great growth and change.

As Cesar Chavez once told me, "Bob Kennedy crossed a line that no other American politician ever crossed."

Chavez meant that Kennedy took suffering more personally after his brother's murder, and was more willing to do something about it. He was open to experience, and experiencing poverty and hunger moved him to act.

But during most of RFK's lifetime, his reputation was framed by the buzzword "ruthless." When I got to know him, I felt that a mass hallucination of mistaken identity was going on. Reputation can err on the side of vice or virtue.

There is so much counterfeit and cosmetic change by politicians (and pop-culture performers) going on—fake makeovers by experts—that sometimes we don't recognize real, interior transformation when we see it.

And sometimes we can't see through the slickest makeovers and masquerades, when they are legitimized by mass-media glorification, and the stampede of conformity. Popularity can quash doubt and independent thinking, at least for a while.

I feel qualified to take on this corrective Giuliani mission because I have known him since 1983. When he was U.S. Attorney, and I was writing *City for Sale*, we had frequent dinners, talking and laughing late into the night about baseball, the mob, Robert Kennedy, race relations, politics, Brooklyn, history, and boxing. (He has a fine sense of humor.) When the book was published in 1989, Giuliani was among the guests at the book party. Although I did not vote for him in 1989, I did vote for him in 1993. And I covered his administration on a daily basis.

In June 1998, Giuliani presented me with a journalism award at a fund-raiser for Greenwich House. In his introduction, the mayor said kind things, complimenting my integrity and judiciousness on issues where we disagreed. I was pleased that he made the presentation and by his choice of words. Such an evening makes it harder for me to dispute his legend now. It creates a slight undertow of restraint and residual liking.

In 1999 I wrote a column suggesting the city build a statue to commemorate the cross-racial friendship between Brooklyn Dodgers Jackie Robinson and Pee Wee Reese. Giuliani called me up and promised to do it, and to put it in Brooklyn. When he announced the statue at a City Hall press conference, he invited me to attend, and gave me more credit than I deserved for the idea.

So I certainly have no dislike for Giuliani in a personal sense. I just think the camera has made him seem bigger than he really is. The *perspective* is what is bogus. I argue this point of view even though I do see a certain softness that has come into Giuliani since 9/11, since he left office. This is a hopeful sign. But it does not erase all the harsh policies and words during his years as mayor. Especially since he does not admit mistakes or issue apologies.

Bertolt Brecht said we should pity the land that needs

heroes. What I'm saying here is that Giuliani was not a hero in the classic sense. He did his job brilliantly on September 11, demonstrating calm, discipline, and delivering the right words at a time of fear and chaos. Individuals he loved dearly died in the attack.

But what he did does not make him a hero on an historical scale. A hero has nobility of character, longevity, a high purpose, selflessness, physical or moral courage, and an original idea that helps humankind.

The authentic heroes of 9/11 are the firefighters, police officers, emergency medical personnel, and the rescue workers from the hard-hat construction unions. They risked their lives to save others. They clawed the twisted debris for months, breathing contaminated air, searching for body parts and DNA evidence.

More than 60 of the 343 dead firefighters were off-duty, racing into smoke and danger when they didn't have to. One of the 23 NYPD officers who died was a policewoman named Moira Smith. She was last seen leading terrified, ash-covered office workers to safety, just before she went back into the doomed towers.

To mislabel a politician as a hero—*as the biggest hero*—demeans the sacrifice, courage, and professionalism of all the genuine heroes and heroines of 9/11.

Among the genuine heroes of that day were the 37 passengers, 5 flight attendants and 2 pilots who attacked the hijackers on United Flight 93. They faced death with courage.

The plane crashed into an open field outside Shanksville,

Pennsylvania, and all aboard were killed. But this mutiny prevented the hijackers from crashing the plane into the White House.

Todd Beamer, one of the hero mutineers, signaled the passengers' revolt by saying, "Let's roll," a rallying cry that became a Neil Young song. Another hero of that day was Reverend Mychal Judge, the chaplain of New York's Fire Department, who died in the ruins, administering to the firefighters. Father Judge lived the life of a selfless saint.

Rudy Giuliani was not really the "Person of the Year" in 2001, as *Time* magazine declared him to be. He saved no lives, found no escape routes in the dark with an ax, carried no one to safety on his back, lifted no beams, discovered no remains. And he had no emergency plan in place in advance to coordinate the police and fire response to such a murderous sneak attack on civilians.

If *Time* magazine wanted a symbolic representation of America's resistance to terrorism, of our national spirit, they might have considered Todd Beamer, or Father Mychal Judge.

My aim in these pages is to try to disentangle Giuliani the superhero myth from the man in full.

But even as I write, I can see the myth growing, and the full man becoming more of a blur.

There is an element of mania now to Giuliani's popularity. Which is to say there is an element of fad and herd instinct. People cheer for him because they have seen others cheer for him on television. People think of him as a hero because America desperately needed a hero after such a heartbreaking catastrophe as 9/11, which ended our national sense of invulnerability.

In July 2002, Giuliani received special permission from Major League Baseball to sit on the bench with the American League team during the all-star game in Milwaukee.

He was the only civilian nonathlete allowed to sit with Garciaparra, Jeter, and Clemens, getting his iconic status ratified with an introduction from the field during the first inning that elicited a roaring ovation.

In August 2002, Giuliani was cheered at the raucous MTV music awards by the apolitical fans of Eminem, Nelly, and Michael Jackson.

During the summer and fall of 2002, Giuliani traveled the country, from Maine, to Florida, to Kentucky, to California, raising money for Republican candidates. Tom Davis, the chair of the National Republican Congressional Committee said, "He is the hottest political property we have, outside the president."

NBC-TV is making a two-hour television movie about Giuliani, scheduled to go on the air in February 2003. The USA Network is also preparing a Giuliani docudrama.

In September 2002, Giuliani told Joyce Purnick of the *New York Times*, "Probably I will be back in politics."

Each week the myth becomes more "persistent, persuasive, and unrealistic."

And when a myth becomes a mania, our democracy needs information to sober up.

2.
The First Amendment

*Congress shall make no law . . . abridging the freedom of speech, or
of the press; or the right of the people peaceably to assemble, and to
petition the Government for a redress of grievances.*

—The Bill of Rights

The Bill of Rights is a sacred text. It is the sec-
ular equivalent of the Ten Commandments and the
Sermon on the Mount.

The concepts of freedom of speech, freedom of the
press, and freedom of religion are what made the United
States a new thing in the world. These concepts of
Madison and Jefferson, which did not exist in Europe, are
still what makes America the greatest country on earth.
These individual freedoms are our civic creed and the
foundation of representative democracy.

"The right to protest for right is the root of the civil-
rights movement," Martin Luther King, Jr. told me in 1967.
"The Voting Rights Act of 1965 became law because we had
freedom of assembly, freedom of speech, and freedom of the
press. Without these rights, we would not have been able to
march triumphantly from Selma to Montgomery."

Rudy Giuliani was a lawyer who defended the First Amendment when he was in private practice from 1977 to 1980. He went to school on the opinions written by liberal Justices Brandeis, Douglas, and Brennan. During those years, as a partner in the Manhattan law firm of Patterson, Belknap & Webb, Giuliani's clients included the Chicago Tribune Company, which owned the New York *Daily News,* and Dow Jones, which owned the *Wall Street Journal.*

Giuliani's specialty was the First Amendment. He did trial litigation defending libel suits. When I got to know him well, during the 1980s, he seemed proud of this role, extremely knowledgeable about the nuances of First Amendment law, and quite passionate about being the custodian of rights handed down from Madison and Jefferson to his corporate clients. Defending the First Amendment seemed more than just a job to Giuliani in his younger days. He professed a reverence for the Founding Fathers' ideals of liberty.

But as mayor, he repeatedly violated these ideals he once advocated fervently. As mayor, he lost more than twenty-five lawsuits, where the courts ruled Giuliani to be in violation of provisions of the First Amendment. This was much more than any other mayor in the history of New York.

Giuliani's tramplings on constitutional rights had a combination of political and psychological motives. Intellectually, he had to know better.

On the political side, opportunism and poll-based calculations were probably a factor. By 1998, facing term limits, impressed by Republican control of the House of

Representatives and the governor's mansion in Albany, and thinking of running statewide for the Senate in 2000, Giuliani began to position himself to be more acceptable to upstate conservatives.

His unconstitutional attacks on museums, artists, activists, racial minorities, the homeless, city employees, taxi drivers, advocacy groups, and the Socialist Workers Party's petitioning in a public park, were all popular among Republican voters and donors outside New York City. His losing all these cases in the courts did not hurt his standing at all among Buffalo and Rochester Republicans. His eye was on a more distant ideological constituency. And on a national fund-raising base among right-wing fat cats in California and around the country.

Art Eisenberg is the senior attorney on the staff of the New York Civil Liberties Union (NYCLU). He wrote several *amicus curiae* (friend of the court) briefs opposing Giuliani in First Amendment cases won by the NYCLU. Eisenberg told me:

> I actually happened to see a Giuliani fund-raising letter he sent to residents of Minnesota. It was in 1999, and Rudy was trying to use his attempt to censor art at the Brooklyn Museum as his emotional appeal to the far right wing. Here I was, involved in trying to stop this censorship, and discovering this appeal for campaign money based on the fact that he was stifling free expression. His fund-raising

letter was boasting about what he was doing in
New York. And it was sent to a right-wing
mailing list in Minnesota. He painted himself
standing up to bigots, and to the "permissive
elitists" backing Hillary Clinton.

(Remember, it was during this same period that Giuliani tried to attack Mrs. Clinton by linking her to what he called a "pro-drug" song by Billy Joel, as part of this cultural war he tried to provoke, to help himself politically outside New York City.)

An aside and a stipulation: The "Sensation" exhibit at the Brooklyn Museum of Art was trashy and in poor taste. It also gave off the huckster's aroma of selling tickets through shock and controversy.

But Giuliani used the exhibit to present himself as a fearless defender of the Virgin Mary. About 40 percent of the statewide electorate in New York is Roman Catholic. Giuliani felt he had to strengthen his image with this constituency before any election against Hillary Clinton, because he was pro–gay rights and pro-choice on abortion.

He did not really care what the New York courts decided. He picked this free speech fight to reposition himself more conservatively in the eyes of upstate and suburban Catholic voters. Giuliani thought an attack on the museum was a no-lose proposition, for a campaign that would never take place.

Richard Emery is a civil-liberties lawyer in private prac-

tice who argued two First Amendment cases against the
Giuliani administration. In one of them he represented
Housing Works, a militant AIDS advocacy group that
Giuliani had de-funded in an act of political reprisal.
Emery told me:

> In a way, Rudy's biggest weakness is that he
> is so smart, so quick on his feet. Therefore,
> Rudy thinks he always knows more than anyone
> else. And that he is never wrong, and that his
> position always has moral rectitude. But this
> can't be true, given the range of expertise
> and specialization you need to govern such a
> complex city as New York.
>
> Because Rudy thinks he is smarter than
> everyone else, he didn't delegate authority as
> mayor. He never deferred to anyone else's
> expertise or experience. The lawyers working
> for him could never tell him he was wrong. He
> didn't tolerate debate within his inner
> circle.

Emery, who voted for Giuliani 1993, went on: "Rudy
eventually became a scary guy. His response to any disagreement was nuclear attack. That's part of the reason
why he constantly overreacted. He had an almost irrational reaction to people and ideas he didn't agree with.
And these were exactly the kind of unpopular ideas that the
First Amendment was created to protect from intolerant

majorities. The First Amendment was drafted to protect dissent by minorities. And Rudy came to not accept this basic principle."

"Intimidation and retaliation became Rudy's philosophy of governing," Emery added.

In his farewell address to the city in December 2001, Giuliani declared "respect for the rule of law" as one of his five guiding principles of leadership.

But judging from his repeated efforts to dilute First Amendment rights, this does not seem to be true. And based on his attempts to repeal term limits for himself and remain in office four more years, or three extra months, following the 9/11 catastrophe. This violation of due process and equal protection, this attempt to change the rules of an election in the middle of the contest, was ultimately abandoned because of resistance. But it disclosed a disrespect—not a respect—for the rule of law.

Giuliani's violations of the First Amendment suggest a fundamental deficit of commitment to pluralism, democracy, the rights of minorities to dissent, and ideological diversity.

"There is an equality of status in the field of ideas," the Supreme Court has observed, "and government must afford all points of view an equal opportunity to be heard."

As mayor, Rudy Giuliani did not adhere to this standard.

The Brooklyn Museum case is the most glaring and legally significant example of Giuliani's unconstitutional bullying; I will return to this rich narrative of folly shortly.

But first let me summarize some of the lesser-known twenty-seven First Amendment lawsuits that the NYCLU won—or helped win—in court against Giuliani. These cases reveal an astonishing pattern of attempted erosions of freedom.

What is alarming is the *volume* and *variety* of these desecrations of the Bill of Rights. They should make the reader tremble at any prospect of Giuliani's becoming Attorney General of the United States, or Director of the FBI, or the czar of homeland security.

Housing Works v. Police Commissioner Howard Safir: The NYCLU disputed the constitutionality of various city policies limiting the size of demonstrations at City Hall— or banning them entirely—while exempting events approved by Giuliani, like rallies honoring his beloved New York Yankees on the steps of City Hall, from these arbitrary restrictions.

The federal courts sided with the NYCLU and issued a permanent injunction against Giuliani's double standard for the right of assembly in April 2000. Giuliani did not appeal. Housing Works is a militant AIDS advocacy group that was often critical of Giuliani. The group wanted to demand more funding for AIDS treatment in the city's budget.

In a separate case involving Housing Works, federal judge Allen Schwartz ruled that aides to Giuliani had deliberately changed the group's rating from a favorable level to deprive it of $2.5 million in federal funds from HUD.

Judge Schwartz restored the funding, and wrote in his

69-page opinion: "The court concludes that the volumi-
nous facts in the record evince well-documented circum-
stantial evidence of retaliatory intent." Schwartz wrote the
reprisal was for free speech, "criticism of the Giuliani
administration."

Housing Works' lawyers Richard Emery and Matt
Brinkerhoff had produced a mayoral staff memo about
Housing Works that said, "Fran hates them," a reference
to Deputy Mayor Fran Reiter. Giuliani himself had called
Housing Works, "a suspect group."

This case documented Giuliani using his mayoral
power as a sword of personal revenge, even before he
tried to do the same thing by de-funding and evicting the
Brooklyn Museum.

Marten v. *Giuliani:* This suit challenged the NYPD's
policy of holding in jail for arraignment—usually
overnight—any individual charged with a minor offense
*if the police alleged this offense occurred during a protest
demonstration.* Shortly after the NYCLU filed its papers,
the Police Department rescinded this policy of harassment. Pamela Marten was an investment banker and a
board member of NOW.

Walton v. *Safir:* This suit challenged the April 1999 dis-
missal from the NYPD of Yvette Walton, a black police
officer who, in the aftermath of the fatal shooting of the
unarmed Amadou Diallo by four white officers, voiced
her beliefs. The black cop spoke out against "racial profiling" by the NYPD's Street Crime Unit, whose members
shot Diallo forty-one times. The federal district court

ruled in November 2000 that the NYPD had fired the officer in revenge for her free speech comments about profiling. In July 2001, the federal court ordered the officer reinstated to NYPD employment. Early in 2002, the new police commissioner, Ray Kelly, issued a written order to all commands, banning all racial profiling by the NYPD.

Harmen v. *City of New York:* Challenged the constitutionality of Giuliani's executive orders that required child-welfare employees of the city who wished to speak to reporters about nonconfidential child-welfare matters to obtain the city's consent in advance of any interview. In March 1998, a federal judge found that these executive orders by the mayor violated the First Amendment and struck them down.

Latino Officers Association v. *Safir:* Challenged the constitutionality of an NYPD policy that required police officers who wanted to make public statements about nonconfidential police practices and policies to first notify the NYPD about any planned statements, to obtain the Police Commissioner's permission to make the remarks, and then to report back to the department the content of what was said. In July of 1997, the federal district court held that this policy violated the First Amendment and preliminarily enjoined the NYPD from enforcing it. Eventually a trial was held, and in September of 2001, the district court ruled that the notice and reporting provisions violated the First Amendment.

Latino Officers Association v. *City of New York:* Challenged the legality of the NYPD's refusal to grant NYPD recognition to the organization of Latino officers who had spoken publicly and critically about discrimination and misconduct by the NYPD. In June 1999, the NYCLU won a preliminary injunction, ordering the NYPD to allow the Latino Officers Association to march in NYPD uniforms in public parades, a standard benefit of recognition given to other ethnic groups of police officers. After a trial took place in the spring of 2000, the city agreed to full recognition, and paid the Latino officers damages to settle the case.

Metropolitan Council on Housing v. *Safir:* Challenged the legality of the Giuliani administration's refusal to allow people to sleep on a public sidewalk across from Gracie Mansion (the mayor's residence) as part of a vigil protesting rent increases. In June 2000, the federal district court ruled that Giuliani's policy was in violation of the First Amendment.

Tunick v. *Safir:* Challenged the city's refusal to allow professional photographer Spencer Tunick to shoot a group of nude models on a public street. In July of 1999, the federal district court held that this refusal violated the First Amendment. The city appealed but lost, and the photo shoot took place in June 2000.

New York Magazine v. *City of New York:* The NYCLU supplied an *amicus curiae* brief to support *New York Magazine's* right to display an advertisement on city buses that gently satirized Giuliani. In the ad, *New York Magazine* called itself "Possibly the only good thing in New York Rudy Giuliani hasn't taken credit for." Giuliani forced the

Transit Authority to remove the ad from all its buses. The magazine sued and won. Giuliani appealed and lost. The ad was finally restored, although the taxpayers had to foot the bill for Giuliani's flagrant effort to censor free speech that playfully tweaked his vanity.

Kalke v. *City of New York:* Challenged the enforcement of a Parks Department policy that banned the distribution of free condoms by a church-sponsored HIV/AIDS prevention program. The courts ruled that the city's suppression of this potentially lifesaving program was in violation of the First Amendment.

People v. *Lyons, Sanchez and Schenk:* Challenged the legality of summonses issued to members of the Socialist Workers Party who were peacefully gathering signatures on petitions to get on the ballot in a public park. A Bronx criminal court judge ruled that the summonses violated the First Amendment, dismissed them, and ordered the NYPD property clerk to return literature seized by the police.

Million Youth March v. *Safir:* In 1999, a fringe hate group led by Khallid Mohammed was denied a permit for a public rally on Labor Day weekend. The city decreed no rally could take place at all; the year before a permit had been negotiated, for a limited time and space. The NYCLU submitted an *amicus* brief, and the federal district court ruled the city could not prevent a group from holding a public rally, which then took place without violence.

Fifth Avenue Presbyterian Church v. *City of New York:* Challenged the legality of the police to threaten to arrest homeless people who were sleeping on church property and chasing them to other locations. The church approved of the homeless sleeping in their doorway as part of the church's policy of helping the homeless.

The NYCLU went into federal court during Giuliani's last month in office and won a temporary restraining order barring the police from entering church property to roust the homeless, or use the threat of arrest to coerce them into leaving that sanctuary.

The homeless who were chased told reporters they were just being harassed to move to less affluent and less visible locations.

In his farewell address, Giuliani attacked the judge who made this decision, saying he was "having a hard time thinking through the ideology that he brings when analyzing his decision."

Giuliani tried to convey the impression that he was pro- tecting the homeless from the winter cold and dispatching them to a warm shelter. But, in fact, the police were just harassing them into less visible shadows on the street, probably so tourists would not see them during the Christmas season.

It was Rudy Giuliani's press secretary, Sunny Mindel, who got him to focus on the "Sensation" exhibit at the Brooklyn Museum of Art, by putting the 200-page catalog for the show in Giuliani's hand, urging him to read it, in the third week of September 1999.

Page 133 featured a work by African artist Chris Ofili,

depicting the Virgin Mary as an African woman with a smear of elephant dung near her left breast. Cutouts of vaginas and anuses floated around her.

"This is fucking outrageous!" the mayor of New York roared to six of his top aides. "This is not art. I'm not going to fucking pay for this!"

Giuliani, who had the fanatic's taste for holy wars, had suddenly found his next jihad against the infidels. Later that day, and again the next day, Giuliani warned the Brooklyn Museum to cancel the show—scheduled to open in ten days—on October 2—or else he would de-fund the museum, cancel its lease with the city, and oust its trustees.

Giuliani had no legal basis to do any of this, so he grasped at a straw. Perhaps as a publicity stunt, the museum had announced that no one under seventeen would be admitted to the exhibit, unless accompanied by a guardian.

In a bit of sophistry, Giuliani claimed this violated the First Amendment rights of those under seventeen. He was using a First Amendment debating point to butcher the intent of Jefferson and Madison. From day one of this drama, he seemed off his game, borderline irrational.

"I'm not going to have any compunction about putting them out of business," Giuliani said of the Brooklyn Museum, which housed the second-largest art collection in the nation.

The mayor called in his commissioner of cultural affairs, Schuyler Chapin, and directed him to tell the museum's director, Arnold Lehman, the city would cancel its $7 million annual budget allocation to the 173-year-old museum, if the institution didn't cave in immediately.

Chapin, a lover of the arts and a believer in artistic freedom, tried to convince the mayor and his deputies that they were embarked on a losing and unconstitutional course.

"We *want* a nuclear explosion," Deputy Mayor Joseph Lhota told Chapin.

"Well, you're going to get it," the cultural affairs commissioner shot back. And he was right.

The Brooklyn Museum was not intimidated the way so many of Giuliani's other foes had been. The museum's trustees may even have wanted this confrontation as much as the mayor did, knowing it would produce an avalanche of free publicity and long lines of paying customers.

The battle was joined when the museum retained Floyd Abrams, the nation's most respected First Amendment lawyer, to present its case to the courts. And Abrams got in the first blow, filing a preemptive lawsuit against Giuliani and the city government, based on First Amendment rights.

The same day the suit was filed (September 28), the museum also lifted the age restriction Giuliani was hyping into a cause, replacing it with a simple sign warning parents "of the challenging content of certain of the works."

At this point, Giuliani had already lost seventeen First

Amendment lawsuits, and the city's arts community and cultural institutions felt they had to take a stand.

It was not easy getting the establishment types who run the city's museums into a consensus to combat this vindictive mayor. One of their leaders said it was "like herding cats."

But in Floyd Abrams, they had a litigator equal to the mayor in intellect and resolve. On the day he filed his papers, Abrams told me:

> There is no obligation from the city to fund the arts. But the First Amendment says, according to a wide, sustained, continuing body of case law, that the funding process may not be used to coerce institutions such as the Brooklyn Museum to do the bidding of its political leaders. So while New York never has to fund any museum, once New York starts down that road, it cannot violate the First Amendment by process of coercion, sanction, threats, retribution and the like.

This was a true, nuanced, and irrefutable analysis of the First Amendment.

Giuliani, meanwhile, went on one of his venom binges. He called press conferences and attacked the museum and its leaders day after day. On these binges, he lost all sense of complexity and proportion.

One day at City Hall, he said, "This show should

happen in a psychiatric hospital, not a museum." A few days later he called the exhibit "pedophiles on parade."

The Giuliani inner circle of ex-prosecutors began to leak stories that the museum's director, Arnold Lehman, was anti-Catholic. This so angered Giuliani's commissioner, Schuyler Chapin, that he said, "We're not going to have Joseph Goebbels in 1999! We are just not going to have it!"

Most reporters assumed Chapin would be fired for insubordination, but he managed to keep his job.

On September 30, I published a column in the *New York Post*. I felt the artworks ranged from mediocre to trash, but that they had to be defended under the First Amendment. I also felt some of it was anti-Catholic, and tried to put myself in the position of a Catholic whose feelings were injured, before I composed my defense of free speech. This is what I wrote:

"When this controversy began, I tried to imagine how I would feel if the offending art was anti-Semitic. If it violated a Jewish icon, how would I really feel?

"I tried to imagine a painting that depicted Anne Frank fornicating with Eichmann. A sculpture mocking the gas chambers of Auschwitz. Dung on Golda Meir.

"I would like to think I would still oppose censorship and defend free expression."

The next day, the *Daily News* published the results of a poll the paper had commissioned: 60 percent of the city supported the Brooklyn Museum, 30 percent backed Giuliani.

Catholics favored the museum 48 percent to 42 percent.

That same day, a full-page advertisement appeared in

the *New York Times* condemning Giuliani's blatant disregard for freedom of speech.

Among the signers were Joan Didion, E. L. Doctorow, Eve Ensler, Mary Gordon, Norman Mailer, Arthur Miller, William Styron, Kurt Vonnegut, Calvin Trillin, Rob Reiner, Susan Sarandon, Kwame Anthony Appiah, Tony Kushner, Joyce Carol Oates, Eric Bogosian, Spalding Gray, John Guare, and Elizabeth Hardwick. The intellectual community felt threatened by this assault on free expression itself.

New York City's leading lay Catholic politician, Council Speaker Peter Vallone, also spoke up in defense of the First Amendment. Vallone, who attends mass every morning, said he found some of the artworks anti-Catholic, and "abhorrent," but still could not support de-funding the museum as punishment, or "setting ourselves up as censors."

Once the case got into the courts, Giuliani cut back on his daily attacks of the museum. But when Hillary Clinton, after several days of silence, belatedly defended free speech, Giuliani responded demagogically, "She agrees with using public funds to attack and bash the Catholic religion."

If Giuliani had just expressed his own opinion of the exhibit and urged a boycott, there would have been no media frenzy and no lawsuit. But he didn't seem to recognize any boundary between his personal emotions and the Constitution. He was putting his polarizing (and backfiring) campaign strategy ahead of the rule of law.

Rudy Giuliani seemed to be running against his own

city, which had been a safe haven for creative artists since before the Civil War, when Walt Whitman began writing his epic poems in Brooklyn.

For more than 150 years, New York City was the mecca that beckoned artistic pioneers because of its atmosphere of toleration, diversity, stimulation, and experimentation. New York's oxygen of free expression had given life to bebop, abstract expressionism, Method acting, the modern protest-folksong revival, the independent film movement, and hip-hop music.

New York was the diverse place that artistic explorers migrated to in their exuberant youth. Edna St. Vincent Millay came from Camden, Maine; Hart Crane from Cleveland; Ralph Ellison from Oklahoma; F. Scott Fitzgerald from St. Paul; Charlie Parker from Kansas City; Duke Ellington from Washington, D.C.; Miles Davis from East St. Louis; Paul Newman from Cleveland; Marlon Brando from Omaha; Elia Kazan from Turkey as a boy; Tennessee Williams from New Orleans; Bob Dylan from Hibbing, Minnesota; Langston Hughes from Cleveland; Bix Beiderbecke from Davenport, Iowa; H. L. Mencken from Baltimore; and Damon Runyon from Denver.

New York's emancipating environment had nurtured native-born giants like Eugene O'Neill, Irving Berlin, Aaron Copland, George Gershwin, Lorenz Hart, Leonard Bernstein, James Baldwin, Norman Mailer, Martin Scorsese, Robert DeNiro, and Al Pacino. Frank Sinatra, Lenny Bruce, Philip Roth, and Allen Ginsberg had grown up within twenty-five miles of New York.

Rudy Giuliani was sticking his thumb in the eye of this rich hometown tradition. He could not expand his love of opera to other, more populist art forms.

The "Sensation" exhibit opened on October 2, and 13,000 people waited on line to see its forgettable contents.

The next morning, Rudy Giuliani, mayor of New York, was the hot-button star on three national political interview shows: NBC's *Meet the Press*, ABC's *This Week*, and *Fox News Sunday*.

Giuliani was getting what he thought he wanted: saturation national exposure. By pre-taping some of his appearances, he was on three networks at the same time.

But Giuliani came across as the intolerant successor to Jesse Helms, as America's new arts-bashing censor.

There was an irony to watching his performances that Sunday morning. Giuliani had once told me he was first attracted to politics by seeing John Kennedy become America's first Catholic president in 1960, conquering bigotry and stereotype. Giuliani felt JFK had opened a door for him, to become America's first Italian Catholic president. Now he was sounding bigoted, and authoritarian, just like the man John Kennedy had to defeat in that 1960 election: Richard Nixon.

On November 1, 1999, U.S. District Court Judge Nina Gershon ruled in favor of the Brooklyn Museum on every issue in dispute.

Judge Gershon ordered Giuliani to stop withholding

city funding from the museum, and to end an eviction proceeding the city had begun.

Judge Gershon wrote: "There is no federal constitutional issue more grave than the effort by government officials to censor works of expression, and to threaten the vitality of a major cultural institution as punishment for failing to abide by governmental demands for orthodoxy."

Judge Gershon ruled that Giuliani had attempted to "coerce" the museum by depriving it of funding—the same point Floyd Abrams had made to me on the day he filed his lawsuit.

Gershon granted a preliminary injunction that barred Giuliani from "taking steps to inflict any punishment, retaliation, discrimination or sanction" that violated the First Amendment.

The decision was a message to curators and museum directors around the country that politicians could not tell them what art to hang, and could not use funding power to punish decisions they did not like.

Giuliani was not a gracious loser. An hour after the ruling was made public, the mayor told the assembled reporters in Schenectady, where he was campaigning for the Senate, that Judge Gershon's 38-page decision "is the usual knee-jerk reaction of some judges."

Giuliani went on to characterize Judge Gershon as, "totally out of control," and said she was, "abandoning all reason under the guise of the First Amendment."

In her decision, Judge Gershon had dismissed as

"absurd" Giuliani's claim that if the city could not with-
hold funds, the museum could convert itself into a city-
funded museum of pornography. She also called the city's
attempt to evict the museum for alleged lease violations
bogus, and "purely pretextual."

From beginning to end, Judge Gershon's ruling was a
stirring defense of the First Amendment—and a stern rep-
rimand to a mayor who was trying to shred it.

When Giuliani pronounced the judge "totally out of
control," he should have been looking into the mirror.

In February 2001, Giuliani made one more lawless
lurch for censorship. He announced he was appointing a
"decency commission" to review art in publicly financed
institutions. He even hinted he might appoint Cardinal
Edward Egan of the Archdiocese of New York to the
panel, which seemed completely amorphous in concept
and purpose. In light of the Gershon decision, it certainly
seemed unconstitutional on its face. Most observers
thought the mayor was just venting on a bad day and
would quickly forget about such an impractical idea.

But in early April he actually appointed his decency
commission to sniff out objectionable art. The members
included his personal divorce lawyer Raoul Felder; his
Parks Commissioner Henry Stern; former Nixon White
House lawyer Leonard Garment; and freelance journalist
and Giuliani crony Martin Bergman. It was hardly a dis-
tinguished group. It contained no real artists.

Lawyer Burt Neuborne, of the Brennan Center for Justice at NYU Law School, pithily summed up the eccentric

venture: "If it's intended to have any powers at all, it's unconstitutional. The only way it would be upheld is if it is a fraud."

It turned out to be a fraud. The decency commission petered out into a nullity. There was no attempt to do anything. Its mission was a blur from the start. Giuliani could never define indecency. The mayor was just indulging his frustrations.

By putting his divorce lawyer on the panel, Rudy invited questions about "decency." Here was a married mayor, openly committing adultery with his girlfriend, Judi Nathan, and at the same time, setting himself up as the arbiter of purity and decency for the whole city.

Here was a moralist with a mistress, trying to censor the arts, oblivious to his own pose of self-righteous moral superiority.

3.
Education

Rudy Giuliani came into City Hall knowing what he wanted to do about crime. Law enforcement was his priesthood. He grew up with four uncles who were police officers. He had been a triumphant federal prosecutor. One of his early mentors as a prosecutor was the legendary NYPD detective Carl Bogen, the model for the TV cop Kojak.

Giuliani knew policing in his bones. He liked cops. He read the academic literature. He understood cop culture. He loathed criminals. He had been elected because the fear of crime was the biggest issue, and voters saw him as the tough, strong remedy.

But he did not have the same knowledge, confidence, or interest in public education. It wasn't his passion. He had attended private Catholic high school and college. He had no uncles or aunts who were schoolteachers. Few of his friends had been products of public education. He knew how to run a police precinct, but not a public school.

Coming into City Hall, Giuliani lacked a personal vision of clarity in the area of education. He was not an expert about teaching, learning, curriculum, teacher education, early-childhood development, or school construction. He tended to see education through the prisms he already knew: budget, management, crime fighting.

He also believed the Democratic Party and the unions were somehow to blame for the absence of learning magic in the classroom.

He was a great wartime consigliere to fight crime, but not such a fine peacetime consigliere to fund and reform education.

As a result, during Giuliani's eight years in office, the public school declined by almost every statistical measure.

At the end of Giuliani's second term, the proportion of students able to pass the eighth-grade English test declined to 29 percent. The percentage of students passing this test dropped 6 percent over 4 years.

In the eighth-grade math test, only 29.7 percent of students met the state standard in 2001.

Graduation rates in high school dropped. Class size stagnated. It took months to repair broken windows. A 1999 report by the Board of Education said that more than half of the schools still weren't connected to the Internet.

In some years Giuliani shifted resources from poorer districts to more middle class districts. In 1999, he diverted funds for improving school facilities from the Bronx and Brooklyn (heavily working class and minority) to Staten Island and Queens (more white and middle class), where the borough presidents were his political allies.

In eight years Giuliani's most remembered comment about public education was that the "whole school system should be blown up."

Giuliani tried for eight years to abolish the central Board of Education, but he could not accomplish this goal. Michael Bloomberg would accomplish it in six months, using the trick of being pleasant.

The mayor occasionally said he wanted to make improving schools the top priority of his second term. But he lacked the focus. And he lacked a coherent, consistent philosophy that might have had an effect on what transpired in the classroom between teacher and pupil.

Giuliani had tremendous leadership skills, but not the collaborative style needed to work with the state legislature, the unions, parents, and the communities of color, where 80 percent of the students came from.

After 1998, Giuliani drifted into his dark mood, scapegoating teachers, and the teachers' union, and their president Randi Weingarten. This abuse only undermined morale among teachers. It also created a negotiating stalemate, so that New York's teachers had to work without a raise, or a contract, for the last 15 months of the Giuliani administration. This, in turn, caused some of the best teachers to retire, and forced the system to hire more and more uncertified teachers to fill the vacancies.

Even Michael Bloomberg, who was elected with the help of a powerful TV commercial by Giuliani, nevertheless told me in February 2002: "Giuliani never got his hands around the school system. There is no question it's gotten worse in the last eight years, not better."

Public education is the urban frontier Giuliani should have dedicated himself to. It may be the most important antipoverty program of all—*if* it is funded properly.

But between 1994 and 1997, Giuliani drained more than $2 billion out of the school system. He cut $4.7 billion from the school construction budget in 1999.

While reducing resources, he raised standards for student performance on tests. This placed the kids in a no-win vise.

Giuliani did not have strong national trends running in his favor in education, the way he did with crime and the economy. He did not have a natural instinct for educational policy.

These are reasons he should have applied himself more—not less—to the schools. But he never did. He never got "his hands around the school system."

He had two capable school chancellors—Ramon Cortines and Rudy Crew—and he forced them both out of office, with the brutal politics of insults, leaks, and disparagement. In an area where he was weak, Rudy would not delegate authority to the professionals. He destabilized the system by picking fights.

And these fierce, dirty fights that Giuliani started were never about improving education for the kids in the schools. They were not about getting more financial aid from the state, or increasing parental involvement in the schools, or finding ways to reduce class size. They were not about the substance of education policy. Instead, these Giuliani brawls were about cultural issues, or about church-state separation questions, or power struggles over control.

To others in the school system, or in government, they did not seem to justify jihads. They seemed to be resolvable by reason and compromise. They didn't have to end with three capable chancellors being driven out of the city, virtually never to return again.

In 1993, while Giuliani was still a candidate for mayor, his campaign participants—Ninfa Segarra and Mike Patrides—who were also on the Board of Education—supplied the deciding votes to fire Joseph Fernandez as chancellor. The reason was that Fernandez had introduced a multicultural curriculum, designed to teach tolerance for gays, to kids as young as first and second grade.

Ramon Cortines would be driven out in 1995 because he wasn't firing employees fast enough and because he was resisting Giuliani's plan to place school security under the control of the NYPD.

Rudy Crew would be driven out in 1999 because he disagreed with Giuliani's newly acquired position in favor of school vouchers; Crew had a principled objection to vouchers.

With these disruptions, and lack of continuity, public education became a lost opportunity under Giuliani.

The New York school system was a dysfunctional mess long before Rudy Giuliani became mayor.

Over decades the system swung back and forth between governance structures based on centralization, and decentralization, with neither concept proving to be more productive than the other.

Mayor Lindsay implemented a decentralization system that created thirty-two community school boards. But these local fiefdoms soon became patronage rackets. The community boards in the minority areas of Brooklyn and the Bronx became corrupt, and dozens of small-time politicians eventually went to prison.

There were school-board elections every three years in which fewer than 2,000 people voted. But these local boards controlled jobs, money, and, in some cases, sold assistant principalships for $5,000. One Bronx school-board member was convicted of stealing a piano out of one public school.

For decades, the state legislature underfunded the city's schools, adding to the chaos. New York City gets 34 per cent of state education funding, even though it has 37 percent of the students.

In August 2002, the nonpartisan Education Trust released a study of education funding in all 50 states. It found that New York has the greatest disparity of funding for schools in poor urban areas in the whole country. New York's schools receive $2,152 *less* per student from the city and state government sources than schools with the fewest neediest pupils. In Illinois—the state with the second-highest disparity—the poorest schools received $2,060 less per pupil.

The nationwide epidemic of crime and drugs during the 1980s did not stop at the schoolhouse door in New York. There were lunchroom killings and playground shoot-outs, one of them killing a beloved principal in Brooklyn.

Even before Giuliani arrived, there was a rapid turnover in school chancellors—four in seven years, at one point. The two most gifted had their terms cut short. Anthony Alvarado had to resign after he had borrowed money from subordinates. Richard Green died from a heart attack brought on by chronic asthma at the age of fifty-two. And during this period more and more middle-class families were choosing to leave the public-school system when their kids reached middle school or move out of the city to the suburbs. By the end of the 1980s, there were only three or four public high schools in the whole city that middle-class families would send their kids to. Almost anyone with money sent their children to private high schools, if they didn't pass the test to get into Bronx Science, Stuyvesant, or Hunter High.

When Rudy Giuliani came into office he inherited a failing, balkanized, dysfunctional school system.

But in some ways he made it even worse, mostly by using chancellors as punching bags. These media muggings, played out over long stretches of time on television and in the newspapers, defined Giuliani's legacy in terms of public education. The media feasts on conflict between personalities, and Giuliani threw the tabloids raw meat.

The money-starved school system needed a leader to fight *for* it—not *with* it.

His chancellor bashing overshadowed everything else because Giuliani made it so dramatic and relentless. None of it was done in private, behind closed doors, as in the old days. He made it a theater of cruelty.

And by the time Giuliani chased his third chancellor out of town, he made it impossible to attract any quality educators to come to New York and take the job with no security, and no guarantee of dignity.

Giuliani made public education a blood sport in New York. The losers were the city's 1.1 million kids and 1,100 public schools

The Board of Education voted 4-to-3 to appoint Ramon Cortines to be the new schools chancellor during the mayoral campaign summer of 1993. The four members who voted for Cortines were all allied with Giuliani. His biggest booster was Mike Patrides, who was both a board member and a high-ranking strategist in the Giuliani campaign.

Cortines, sixty-two, had been a lifelong educator in California, managing three different school systems. He was awaiting confirmation to be the undersecretary for education in the Clinton administration when he agreed to take the job in New York.

Cortines was a thoughtful, hardworking reformer. His personality was that of a stiff loner. He was all business. He was not a backslapper, or a cocktail-party animal, or a storyteller. He was aloof, methodical, and did not let people get close to him. He was at his desk every morning at 6:00 A.M. making his own coffee, and his own phone calls.

"Trying to make urban school districts perform better is what I find exciting," Cortines told me in an early interview. A friend called him "a scientist of learning."

Before Cortines arrived in New York, he had been "outed" as gay by a San Francisco publication. He would never comment on his sexual orientation once he arrived in New York. It was private—like everything else about him.

Fernando Ferrer, the Bronx borough president, did not support Cortines at first. He was not pleased that the pro-Giuliani faction on the Board of Education had chosen him while Dinkins was still mayor, and Dinkins' two appointees had voted against him.

But in a recent interview, Ferrer described how he changed his mind.

"Cortines won me over within six months," Ferrer told me. " I came to recognize he was a good manager and a genuine reformer. He was actually cutting the bloat out of the bureaucracy—in a sensible way. Cortines had a vision. He was innovative and smart. He won me over with his performance in office."

Rudy Giuliani, whose campaign cohorts had recruited Cortines to come to New York, did not see the new chancellor as a reformer. He saw him as an obstructionist, as too independent.

There was no personal chemistry between Cortines and

Giuliani's team of flame-throwing, tough-guy ex-prosecutors. They did not speak the same vocabulary. Giuliani himself was not comfortable with Cortines, the gentle introvert.

In early 1994, Giuliani started his brusque demands that Cortines fire 2,500 people from the staff of the central Board of Education. The mayor had to make some big budget cuts, and he was certain there were large numbers of clubhouse patronage hacks idling at their desks, stopping things from happening.

As the new chancellor, going through his first budget cycle, Cortines felt obligated by his institutional position to resist such massive and indiscriminate layoffs of his employees, based on a number that seemed plucked out of the air.

April 1994 brought a classic Giuliani showdown confrontation. Cortines was summoned—alone late in the evening—to come immediately to Gracie Mansion, to face the mayor and some of his inner circle of former prosecutors. After being made to wait for an hour, the chancellor was finally led into a room to face his interrogators.

Earlier that day, Cortines had agreed to cut about 1,200 positions, some through attrition. But this had angered Giuliani as paltry and temporizing.

At the start of this late night meeting, Giuliani demanded that Cortines fire his press aide, John Beckman, and his top fiscal aide, Leonard Hellenbrand.

Giuliani was angry at Hellenbrand, who had been quoted in the *Times* that morning saying the goal of firing

2,500 people was "not doable." Beckman had worked for Dinkins, and this make his loyalty suspect.

Backed up by his team, the mayor had Cortines cornered and was trying to bully him. He told the chancellor that he had to accept Herman Badillo—Giuliani's unsuccessful 1993 running mate—as the new monitor for the school system, looking over his shoulder, he also had to lay off 2,500 people.

Cortines felt violated, later telling an aide he felt like a suspect taken down to a prosecutor's office without a lawyer and getting worked over by experts.

After an hour of this, Cortines told the mayor he would find 2,500 jobs to eliminate if these layoffs were spaced out over fifteen months. But he said he would not fire Beckman and Hellenbrand. And he would quit as chancellor if Badillo was installed as a monitor.

"I know how to run a school system," he told Giuliani.

Before Cortines left, the Mayor told him his two top deputies would have to be fired by noon the next day.

The next morning Beckman dutifully offered to resign, but Cortines would not let him. Deputy Mayor Peter Powers kept calling from City Hall every half hour, asking if the two targeted aides had been fired yet.

At noon, when Beckman and Hellenbrand had not been fired, Giuliani escalated the war. He simply announced to the press that Badillo was now the monitor for the school system.

When that happened, Cortines asked Beckman to draft a press release announcing his resignation, and to call some select opinion-makers in the media with the news of his departure.

Carol Gresser was the president of the Board of Education. She was an ally of Giuliani and she had voted for Cortines. When she heard that Cortines was quitting after seven months on the job, and when she heard the way he was demeaned at Gracie Mansion, she swung into action, trying to get him to stay.

Gresser thought Cortines was doing an excellent job. And she was starting to get a little irritated by the frequency of Giuliani's attacks on the Board of Education. They were aimed at the institution she was president of.

Gresser called Cortines and asked him to rescind his resignation.

"The children need you," she said.

"I have my integrity," Cortines replied, saying he couldn't remain in the job the way he was being abused.

As a last resort, she called Mario Cuomo, then in his twelfth year as governor and a public figure with unusual skills as a mediator.

As Cuomo recalls it: "I called Cortines up and invited him to come to my office. He came and I listened to him. His feelings were clearly hurt, but he wouldn't say that. He just said he had lost the confidence of the Mayor, that his efficacy was destroyed. I thought he was potentially a very good chancellor and pleaded with him to stay on the job. I thought his quitting would disrupt the system. Then I helped negotiate a truce. Beckman and Hellenbrand could keep their jobs."

That night there was a press conference at Gracie Mansion announcing the truce. Cortines would accept Badillo, as a monitor, and he promised to eliminate 2,500 jobs over a period of time.

The sensitive Cortines never really got over such rough, disrespectful treatment. But Cuomo's brief mediation suggested these wars between the mayor and various chancellors did not have to be the Steel Cage Death Matches that Giuliani made them, with no chance of finding a face-saving, flexible, middle ground.

Even after the Board of Education voted to give Cortines a new two-year contract, Giuliani only intensified his vituperation.

Cortines told a legislative hearing, "We are caught in a situation that's almost like—kiss the ring and we'll give you another buck. But if you complain, you may not get the kind of money you need . . . I should not have to go across the river and genuflect to Giuliani."

In May 1995, 10,000 people marched across the river, over the Brooklyn Bridge to City Hall, to protest Giuliani's extreme cuts in the education budget. Union president Sandra Feldman, Board of Education president Carol Gresser, and dozens of politicians marched with parents, teachers, and students.

But Cortines backed out of a decision to participate in the march after a Giuliani intermediary warned Cortines to stay away.

But Cortines did not gain any goodwill with his absence. Giuliani just picked up a new issue for attacking the chancellor. He started demanding that Cortines accept Police Department control of the over 3,000 school safety officers. Day after day the mayor repeated that the NYPD was better qualified to protect the students than Cortines.

"I don't work for the mayor," Cortines told the press. "I work for the Board of Education."

Giuliani responded in a very personal way. He said Cortines was being "precious" about his criticism. He said Cortines should "stop whining." He said Cortines should "stop playing the little victim."

Essentially, Giuliani was right. With crime in the schools increasing by 25 percent, the NYPD was better suited to manage school security.

But there was an edge of sadism in these attacks. And a vague odor of homophobia, even if it was unconscious and inadvertent.

A week later, Cortines resigned for good. He couldn't take the personal battering anymore. He was working eighteen hours a day and getting rewarded for improved reading scores with venomous ridicule.

A few hours after Cortines quit, Giuliani responded with one last kick: "You want my reaction to it? I won't quit."

Four months after he resigned, Cortines and Ed Koch did a joint taped interview with *New York Magazine*. The reporter asked Cortines if Giuliani's choice of words, like "whining" and "precious" and "little victim" had carried an innuendo of sexual orientation.

"I've dealt with innuendo all my life," Cortines answered, and would go no further.

Koch, who suspected there was a whiff of gay-baiting going on, said that "forcing Ray's resignation was the worst thing Rudy did as mayor."

This was said in October 1995, with more than six years to go.

The next schools chancellor was Rudy Crew, a forty-five-year-old black Democrat from Tacoma, Washington. He had charisma, adroit political instincts, and the capacity to inspire. He got the job with Giuliani's blessing.

For three years the two men worked exceptionally well together, becoming close personal friends, smoking cigars together, exchanging holiday gifts, sharing confidences about their troubled marriages, and attending Yankee games.

Crew also did a fine job managing the dysfunctional system. He was more aggressive than Cortines in combating corruption, putting two parasitic Bronx districts under trusteeships. He also secured more arts funding for the schools.

At the same time, he did whatever was necessary to keep the mayor happy. He replaced Hellenbrand with a fiscal analyst from the mayor's office. He negotiated the takeover of school security by the NYPD. He stepped aside and let Giuliani oust Carol Gresser as president of the Board of Education. He agreed to end the policy of "social promotions"—automatic graduation to the next grade.

During the 1997 mayoral election, Crew attacked Giuliani's challenger, Ruth Messinger, for a TV commercial she shot inside a private school that attempted to dramatize public-school overcrowding. His press staff also barred cameras from entering a school where Messinger was speaking.

Reading scores had dropped 5.9 percent in 1996. But they spiked up 3.6 percent in the election year of 1997. Crew had managed this timely statistical uptick by excluding large numbers of non-English-speaking students from taking the standardized test—a little cheating to make the boss look good.

Also, while Giuliani had cut the education budget by $1.3 billion his first three years as mayor, he restored some funding for the re-election–year budget.

The blowup came in the spring of 1999, and the fuse was vouchers for private schools. Giuliani suddenly decided he favored vouchers, even though most experts thought they violated church-state boundaries.

In Crew's first conversation with Giuliani, back in 1995, he had told the mayor about his long history of opposing vouchers—on principle—as harmful to public education.

Giuliani himself was on record as repeatedly opposing a voucher system. As a candidate in 1993, he had told United Federation of Teachers' President Sandra Feldman that he believed vouchers were "unconstitutional."

In May 1995, he told a UFT conference that "vouchers would bleed the public schools of needed funds."

In a speech to the Wharton Club in August 1995, the mayor declared, "Vouchers would weaken, if not create the collapse of the New York City public-school system."

But by January 1999, Giuliani, facing term limits, was seriously thinking about running for the Senate in 2000. His advisers and pollsters were telling him that if he switched his position on vouchers, it would help him with Catholic voters upstate, and the national Republican Party.

So he slipped a favorable reference to a voucher plan into his state of the city address that month.

According to Wayne Barrett's definitive Giuliani biography, *Rudy!*, following this voucher's reference, the mayor told an alarmed Crew, "Don't worry about it. It's just a political thing, a campaign thing. I'm not going to do anything. Don't take it seriously."[1]

But the next month Giuliani sent the City Council a budget modification with $4.5 million for voucher funding. And in his financial plan for the next fiscal year, issued in February, the mayor included $12 million to

---

[1]The following section on the Giuliani-Crew conflict over vouchers relies heavily on Barrett's remarkable account in his book, which Giuliani has never challenged. Barrett told me: "I have never met Rudy Crew. But I did about thirty hours of telephone interviews with him in February and March of 2000. He was living in the state of Washington and I interviewed him for hours on his cell phone. It was almost all on the record. He was eloquent. When my book came out, he called me to say he enjoyed it a great deal. Even though I didn't know him, some intermediaries we knew in common convinced Crew to talk to me."

Full-disclosure reminder: Barrett and I wrote *City for Sale* together. Giuliani the prosecutor was the hero of this 1989 book.

launch a voucher experiment. This was something Crew now had to take seriously.

Crew, who had done almost everything the mayor desired, was now feeling betrayed. He told a *Daily News* editorial writer that he was prepared to resign over the voucher disagreement.

He then told Giuliani he had said this. Giuliani then called the *Daily News*, and what was planned as an anti-voucher editorial became a news story instead.

The mayor immediately began to pressure a new member of the Board of Education—Terri Thomson—to support a voucher plan.

Crew, ever the subtle politician, then backtracked a half step. He told reporters that he would not quit if the voucher plan was run out of City Hall, and if the Board of Education was not "contaminated" by it.

Crew then met with Giuliani and reminded the mayor of his own prior statements opposing vouchers.

"I just changed my mind," Giuliani said. "The change in the schools isn't happening fast enough."

Giuliani made it sound as if vouchers could improve class size, or teacher training, or bilingual education, when it would only drain the already-insufficient budget.

From March till May, the media was consumed by this pointless personal fight over vouchers. The mayor could not accept a friend's feeling bound to a principle of belief.

It was a pointless fight because State Education Commissioner Richard Mills announced on March 4 that it was against the law to use public tax dollars for private tuition. It could not be done under New York's state constitution. It was just political theater, like Giuliani's attempt to censor art at the Brooklyn Museum.

Steven Sanders, the chairman of the New York State Assembly's Education Committee, told reporters, "There is no law that allows for vouchers. In order for this proposal to become law, it requires more than a vote by the Board of Education. It requires a vote by the legislature. And the legislature is not going to pass a law that will commit the use of public money in vouchers for private schools."

The lead *New York Times* editorial on March 5 said:

> Mayor Rudolph Giuliani's renewed push for a school voucher experiment illustrates what can happen when his national political ambitions conflict with the needs of New York City's public schools. A voucher plan could enhance the mayor's image in national Republican circles, but it might also lose him a fine Schools Chancellor. . . .
>
> Chancellor Crew has argued strenuously and correctly that scarce public funds should not be used for private or parochial schools, draining taxpayer support in the process. He also argues that a pilot program would not be a mere experiment, but a bad precedent that could even violate the State Constitution. . . .
>
> Vouchers might give Mr. Giuliani another

```
badge to wear on the national stage, but at an
unacceptable cost if the city loses Chancellor
Crew in the process.
```

On May 2, the *Daily News* published the results of a poll that showed broad public support for Crew. By 55 percent to 39 percent, New Yorkers believed education tax money should only go for public schools. Even Catholics opposed the voucher plan, 48 percent to 43 percent.

Of those polled, 54 percent thought Giuliani was pushing the voucher plan "to improve his chances of getting elected to the U.S. Senate," while only 30 percent thought it was "because he is serious about improving the quality of education."

Crew's overall job performance was approved by 51 percent, while 18 percent disapproved.

It was in April, in the middle of his jihad against Crew, that Giuliani made his infamous remark that "The whole school system should be blown up."

Crew, by then feeling his days were numbered, responded by sending out a fax to hundreds of city leaders, calling Giuliani's comment "reckless" and "destructive."

For the next six months, Giuliani kept up his attacks on Crew and the school system. A report was released about student cheating on standardized tests. A story was leaked about Crew's out-of-town trips. Stories were leaked that Crew's marriage was in trouble.

Under this constant pressure, Crew began to crack a little. When a Giuliani ally on the City Council called for his resignation, Crew ridiculed this Republican's height. He became more aloof. He seemed ground down. He would not tell his allies what he was thinking.

Finally, on December 23, 1999, Giuliani put the four votes together, and Crew was fired by the Board of Education.

A few months after he was fired, Crew spoke extensively with Wayne Barrett about his experience with Giuliani.

On policy substance, Crew said of Giuliani, "He thought schools were a series of episodes, Round One, Round Two. He had no pedagogical commitment, no educational philosophy, no grounding in a belief system."

When it came to the personal and the psychological, Crew spoke with wounded insight. "When Rudy sees a need to take someone out, he has a machine, a room full of henchmen, nicking away at you, leaking crazy stories. He is not bound by the truth. I have studied animal life, and their predator/prey relations are more graceful than his. . . .

"There is a very, very powerful pathology operating inside this man. . . . I believe he feels an anger about some piece of his life that just takes over."

Giuliani's voucher plan never became a reality. There was never a chance it would happen.

What Giuliani was talking about was a blatant violation

of the separation of church and state, under New York's constitution. The state education commissioner, the state legislature, and the City Council were never going to allow it to occur. And Giuliani knew it.

Giuliani ended a constructive working alliance with Crew, and a friendship, for nothing more than posturing for a Senate campaign that never happened.

After six months in office, Michael Bloomberg negotiated mayoral control and accountability over the schools. He did it without blowing anything up, without any psychodrama in the tabloids.

During months of complex private meetings, Bloomberg and his deputies negotiated the abolition of the Board of Education, and the mayor's new power to name one leader for the entire school system.

Bloomberg negotiated this precondition for change with Governor Pataki and the state legislature. And he won the UFT's support.

One reason he was able to do it was that he also won over the legislature's Black and Puerto Rican Caucus during a long meeting at Gracie Mansion. The caucus had never even met with Guiliani as a group the previous eight years.

Some caucus members had opposed abolishing the central Board of Education, and the community school boards, when Giuliani was mayor, partly because he would not return their phone calls or recognize their existence. His shunning had bred their spite.

Bloomberg was able to create a new structure of school governance that had eluded Giuliani for two terms.

Earlier the same month, Bloomberg did something else Giuliani couldn't do. He negotiated a contract with the teachers' union that provided both raises and some productivity improvements. The teachers had been working without a contract for nineteen months. Giuliani had scapegoated the union and attacked teachers to vent his anger. Bloomberg insulted no one, and let his staff work out a complicated deal that included a one-time allotment of state funds.

Bloomberg took ownership of the schools, where Giuliani had used them as a punching bag.

In August 2002, the outgoing chancellor, Harold Levy, held a retreat near Princeton, New Jersey, where he introduced Joel Klein, Bloomberg's new choice to lead the school system, to all the local district superintendents.

One of those superintendents, who had 16 years of seniority, said, "I've never seen one chancellor introduce another."

Rudy Giuliani was not history's Indispensable Man, as he thought he was, following 9/11, when he attempted to repeal term limits for himself, or at least gain an extra ninety days in power.

Michael Bloomberg, with no prior experience in government, has already accomplished educational objectives that Giuliani could not.

For all the times Giuliani spoke the word "reform," he had made himself an impediment to reform, because of what Rudy Crew called his, "very, very powerful pathology."

Anger undermined Giuliani. Anger at Crew, anger at Cortines, anger at unions, anger at minority legislators.

Pathology became his pedagogy.

4.
Race

Snapshot 1967: It is the summer of the Newark and Detroit riots. Rudy Giuliani is at NYU Law School, and is a summer intern at Mudge Rose Guthrie Alexander, John Mitchell's law firm.

Peter King, now a maverick Republican congressman from Long Island, is also an intern at the same law firm. He and Giuliani take the same Long Island commuter train to and from the Manhattan law office each day. This is how King remembers the young Rudy in that summer of racial violence and cities on fire:

> That summer Rudy was like a black militant. He was blacker than the blacks. He told me he supported the rioters, that if he lived in those conditions of poverty and police brutality, he would be a rioter, too.
>
> I remember distinctly one morning riding in on the train, and Rudy is telling me he was drinking the night before in some black bar, and how he got into an argument with a black

guy about the rioting. Rudy called the guy an
'Uncle Tom' and claimed he finally persuaded
the guy that violence was necessary."

Rudy was a very rigid, intolerant leftist,
in those days. He wanted me, and everybody
else, to agree with his point of view about
black militancy.

Snapshot 1989: Giuliani is running for mayor. We had dinner in the middle of the campaign, in June or July. He told me he expected the incumbent mayor, Ed Koch, to win the Democratic primary against David Dinkins. He said he hoped to win at least half the black vote in a general election against Koch, whose administration he had investigated as U.S. Attorney. He was well aware of Koch's attacks on black leaders in his recent book, which contained the false accusation that Basil Paterson had been tolerant of anti-Semitism. He boasted his campaign was more liberal than Koch's on the homeless issue. Giuliani told me one of his intermediaries had been talking to Bill Lynch, Dinkins' campaign manager.

(Lynch later confirmed to me that he had "a couple of meetings" with journalist Marty Bergman, who would later be appointed by Giuliani to his preposterous "decency commission." Lynch says he would not have worked actively for Giuliani against Koch, but other black elected officials say they might have, since Koch was sometimes racially divisive. And if he had defeated Dinkins, there might have been a residue of resentment among some black voters.)

But Dinkins won the primary against Koch. Black teenager Yusef Hawkins had been murdered by a white gang three weeks before the election, just because he had entered the all-white Brooklyn neighborhood of Bensonhurst. This shifted the election. It energized voter turnout in the black community, and made moderate whites think the city needed a healer like Dinkins, more than a polarizer like Koch, in a new climate of tensions.

As soon as Hawkins was killed, on August 23, Reverend Al Sharpton began organizing marches in Bensonhurst, a predominantly Italian-American community. Giuliani defended the legality of these marches, while Koch called for an end to the protests, which were volatile, as white teenagers taunted Sharpton with watermelons and profanity. "There is no racial tension," Koch declared.

Both Giuliani and Koch attended the Hawkins funeral. Giuliani was mildly jeered in the all-black church, but Koch was booed so strongly both inside and outside the packed church that he had to leave through a side door with his police security escort.

Giuliani was courting the black vote until the day Dinkins beat Koch in the primary.

So instead of possibly winning half the black vote against Koch, Giuliani received only a negligible smattering of black votes competing against Dinkins. When Giuliani defeated Dinkins by 50,000 votes in 1993, he received almost no black votes. He entered City Hall resentful of the black community's overwhelming opposition. He was not able to understand that blacks felt the same group pride in Dinkins that Catholics, like himself, had felt with John Kennedy's barrier-breaking victory over anti-Catholic bigotry in 1960.

I believe that this twist of fate—having to run against Dinkins instead of Koch—was the turning point in Giuliani's emotional life about race.

If he had beaten Koch in 1989, with significant black support, everything might have gone in a different direction. His opportunism would have had a positive impact on his racial attitudes, because of black votes for him.

Giuliani thought of himself as a "man of destiny," who was going to be president someday. Losing his first bid for public office, to an African-American he felt superior to, fractured his psyche. His ego had a hard time accepting the judgment of the people.

Snapshot 1992: I am interviewing Giuliani over dinner for an article I am writing for *Playboy*, calling Alfonse D'Amato, "the worst senator in America."

Even though I had supported Dinkins in 1989, Giuliani is still friendly. The interview is valuable. Giuliani describes for me—on the record—how D'Amato twice tried to intervene on behalf of major Mafia figures, while Rudy was U.S. Attorney. One was Gambino godfather Paul Castellano, and the other was Mario Gigante, the brother of Genovese family boss, Vincent "Chin" Gigante. D'Amato had used the sinister mob lawyer, Roy Cohn, as an intermediary.

Over dessert, the conversation turned to Giuliani's defeat in the 1989 election with Dinkins.

"They stole that election from me," Giuliani said with vehemence. "They stole votes in the black parts of Brooklyn, and in Washington Heights. Illegal Dominican immigrants were allowed to vote in Washington Heights."

"And the media was biased against me," Rudy continued. "Dinkins supporters like the *Amsterdam News* called me a fascist and compared me to Mussolini, and none of your liberal friends wrote that was unfair. But whenever I made accurate criticism of Dinkins' ethics, like his not paying his taxes for four years, I was called a racist just for mentioning it. There was a double standard operating against me. A white candidate can't criticize a black candidate in this city without getting defamed as a racist."

Rudy Giuliani grew up in a provincial white world. His family moved from Brooklyn to the suburbs when he was fourteen.

His 1961 graduating class at Bishop Loughlin Memorial High School had only 4 blacks among 378 students. His graduating class at Manhattan College had only 3 blacks out of 744 students.

Yet the best evidence is that, at least intellectually, Giuliani was a liberal about race until he ran for mayor. He once told me he had a poster of Martin Luther King, Jr. in his room while he was in high school. He told me how he stood on line for hours to view Robert Kennedy's casket, after serving as a volunteer in Kennedy's campaign for president in 1968. Giuliani told me that he voted for George McGovern for president in 1972, rather than Richard Nixon.

Some of Giuliani's critics have attributed some of his authoritarian and racially intolerant attitudes to his Catholic education. But I strongly disagree with this theory.

Two of my close friends—Kevin McCabe and Joe Spinelli—both cited in the acknowledgements for this book—attended Bishop Loughlin Memorial High School during the same period as Giuliani. And they are tolerant, pluralistic liberals.

Mario Cuomo is a product of St. John's University, and he is liberal *because of* his religious faith and understanding of theology.

One of the most moral and radical people I know is a Roman Catholic priest—Father John Powis of St. Barbara's Church in Bushwick, Brooklyn.

So I see no cause-and-effect between Giuliani's parochial-school education and his more conservative views as mayor. Growing up, Giuliani was influenced by John and Robert Kennedy, not Joe McCarthy and Cardinal Spellman. He did grow up in an almost all-white world at Loughlin, but so did most white teenagers of that era.

In 1982, Deputy U.S. Attorney General Giuliani played a shameful role in defending the torture and repression by the Duvalier dictatorship in Haiti. He implemented a policy of interdicting boats carrying Haitian refugees seeking freedom, and either sending them back, or detaining them in intolerable internment conditions in Florida.

This may have marked the beginning of his changing

views on race. Certainly, black Haitians fleeing tyranny were treated differently from Cubans who were fleeing Castro.

But Giuliani was not the policy-maker here. President Reagan supported the dictatorship in Haiti. Attorney General William French Smith and the State Department were the architects of the wretched policy Giuliani implemented with gusto. He may have done this to prove himself to the more conservative Reaganites.

My own instinct is that the more likely Rubicon on race was losing the 1989 election against Dinkins. That's when something fundamental changed in Giuliani's heart. After that rejection, Giuliani developed a bitterness, a victim psychology, and perhaps a lust for revenge against the community that thwarted his ambition.

The worm of rancor settled in his soul.

Whatever the timing of the conversion, whatever the root cause, Rudy Giuliani's record on race was a disgrace as mayor of New York. But he was not a racist.

He ran in 1993 on the comforting slogan, "One standard, one city." But he governed by a double standard that helped divide, and then consolidate two cities.

It may even be more accurate to say Giuliani governed with a triple standard, because he treated Latinos somewhat better than blacks, and received more votes from Latinos than blacks in 1993 and 1997.

Giuliani enjoyed a good relationship with some of the sleaziest Latino politicians, many of whom backed him in 1997. But he treated the most thoughtful and inde-

pendent Latino political leaders, like Congressman Jose
Serrano and Bronx Borough President Fernando Ferrer, as
if they were black.

During his first month in office, Giuliani discarded the
affirmative-action plan that had been city policy under
David Dinkins. He stopped advertising job openings in
black newspapers. He ignored a mandate in the City
Charter that he consult with the Equal Employment Practices Commission, a quasi-independent body that was
created to monitor minority hiring.

Giuliani also announced his decision to eliminate New
York City's minority-contracting program, which since
1992 had overseen $270 million worth of contracts
awarded to qualified firms owned by minorities and
women.

A *New York Times* editorial on January 28, 1994, called
the move—in the first month of his term—"wrong-
headed." The *Times* described the program he killed as
"One of the most socially beneficial and cost-effective
programs of its kind anywhere."

These decisions at the outset of his first term sent a
message to his commissioners and administrators that no
one would be looking over their shoulder on the issue of
minority hiring. They could do whatever they wanted.

Every morning at 8:00 A.M. the new mayor met with
his loyal inner circle to plan strategy and make decisions.
There was not one black in this daily meeting. For several
years, its participants were First Deputy Mayor Peter
Powers; Chief of Staff Randy Mastro; Counsel Dennison

Young; Corporation Counsel Paul Crotty; Communications Director Christine Lategano; Budget Director Joe Lhota; Deputy Mayors John Dyson and Fran Reiter; senior advisor Richard Schwartz; and Deputy Mayor Ninfa Segarra.

Like many political leaders, Giuliani was comfortable surrounded by people who were in his own image—who were like him. He liked to be around ex-prosecutors who had worked for him in the U. S. Attorney's office, like Mastro and Young. Powers had been his best friend since high school.

Ed Koch was also most comfortable surrounded by Jews with working-class origins like himself, and with similar politics and cultural taste, like Bess Myerson, Dan Wolf, Henry Stern, Victor Botnick, and David Garth.

Jimmy Carter hired a lot of White House staff from Georgia. JFK had his famous "Irish Mafia" from Massachusetts.

But as a result of the dismantled affirmative action program, fewer blacks were getting jobs in city government, even as the city was becoming more black and Latino.

In March 1996, Michael Powell made an analysis of black employment in top-level jobs for the *New York Observer*. His most striking discovery was that "since Rudolph Giuliani took office, 4,632 fewer blacks worked in agencies under Mayoral control. In contrast, white male employment has edged up by 387.

"The Mayor has appointed 600 additional white officials and administrators; at the same time, the number of senior black officials had decreased by 258. In the Mayor's office, 20 employees earn more than $100,000; one is African-American."

As a candidate in 1993, Giuliani waffled back and forth about affirmative action as a legal concept. After he was elected, he practiced a hiring policy that came close to being discriminatory against blacks. It was certainly discriminatory.

Giuliani often said that his favorite mayor in New York history was the passionate populist Fiorello La Guardia, who governed the city colorfully and competently for three terms, from 1934 to 1945. Giuliani kept a picture of La Guardia in his office and invoked his legacy at every opportunity.

But *Newsday* columnist Joseph Dolman once asked La Guardia's biographer Thomas Kessner to compare the two Italian-American mayors.

"LaGuardia did not have a permanent disagreement with a whole part of the city," Kessner replied, making the essential distinction.

Two of Giuliani's original appointees had severely disturbed attitudes about race: Deputy Mayor for Economic Development John Dyson and Parks Commissioner Henry Stern.

Dyson was probably just an arrogant elitist. But I would have to say, based on personal experience, that Stern was a racist and never should have been appointed.

In 1978, Stern told me that he believed that blacks

were "genetically inferior, because they have smaller brainpans." Other people heard similar remarks by Stern, who was not discreet about his ideas.

Dryson was an odd choice to be deputy mayor. He was a millionaire who lived in upstate Millbrook, where his family owned a winery. He never lived in New York City. He never changed his voting address to the city. He took a helicopter most Fridays back to his home, two hours away. Dyson once famously said he had "the normal disregard" for New York City, revealing his own clueless, eccentric snobbery.

Dyson got his appointment through Liberal Party boss Raymond Harding. He had helped finance Harding's successful campaign to regain control of the organization that was neither liberal nor a real political party; it was a patronage mill that provided a line on the ballot. It had given that line to Giuliani in 1989 and 1993. Giuliani would give top jobs to both of Harding's sons, one of whom was quite able, and the other totally unqualified and later became involved in a scandal. And as state power commissioner, Dyson had hired Harding's wife. It was all patronage favor-trading.

Five weeks into Giuliani's term, a memo written by Dyson was leaked to the *Daily News*. The memo was mostly a bunch of conservative ideas, from eliminating parole, to appointing a "revolutionary with a smile" to make welfare recipients work. Dyson called the welfare system "shrink think."

This memo (written in December, the day after Dyson

was appointed) began by reassuring Deputy Mayor Peter Powers: "Do not worry. Two white guys have been running this city of immigrants for over 200 years!"

This was in response to a story in the *Daily News* that raised questions about whether Powers and Giuliani could govern "an increasingly diverse immigrant city."

Given what would happen during the next eight years, the article asked the right question, and Dyson's memo was the first evidence there would be problems of insensitivity coming from an administration with no blacks with daily access to the mayor to give him input and another perspective, for the first few years.

In July 1994, Dyson caused another racial flare-up.

Comptroller Alan Hevesi was trying to retain a black-owned financial management firm to advise the city on bonds, pensions, and investments.

Dyson and Giuliani opposed retaining the black-owned firm, and Dyson told a reporter that Hevesi "ought to know a bid from a watermelon."

Most blacks and many whites interpreted the reference to a watermelon in this context as a racial slur. Peter Vallone, the white moderate City Council Speaker from Queens, said Dyson's crack was "clearly a racist statement." He demanded that Dyson apologize or be removed from office. (Vallone was a rival of Hevesi's, and they would both run for mayor in 2001 and lose in the primary.)

"You can interpret it either way you want," Giuliani said, while denying the watermelon image was a racial slur.

Dyson left the administration in April 1996, never fully fitting in the prosecutorial, workaholic, subordinate, super-loyal culture of the Giuliani inner circle that others named "the yes, Rudys."

In April 1999, twenty black and Latino employees of the Parks Department filed a complaint with the federal Equal Employment Opportunity Commission (EEOC). They charged their boss, Henry Stern, with a pattern of discrimination in promotions, and reprisals against those who complained. Almost all the plaintiffs were still working for Stern and had seniority.

The Parks Department has 2,000 full-time employees and operates 1,700 parks, playgrounds, pools, and recreational facilities. At the time the complaint was filed, more than half of the department's employees were black or Latino—but not one of the twenty-five highest-paid executives and managers was black! Minorities dominated the lower-paying jobs; there was a "glass ceiling" when it came to promotions, to jobs paying above $70,000 a year.

This is the story of plaintiff Walter Beach, who was the chief of recreation for Brooklyn until he was fired in May 1999, after making complaints about racism in the Parks Department. Beach was the highest-ranking black line manager under Stern; he made $59,000 a year.

In 1997 Beach says he attended a going-away party for one of his employees, who was leaving to attend Yale University. Speaking at the party, Stern said the young man would be going to school with "people like Rockefellers and duPonts, as well as the quota kids."

Beach was hurt by this gratuitous derogatory comment about minority students, and expressed his concern to his supervisors.

As commissioner, Stern has a strange policy of requiring all employees who had contact with him to accept nicknames. Beach declined to accept a nickname that would be put on a name tag. He explained to Stern that his great-grandfather was the first man in the family not born into slavery, and that he had the name Walter, that his father and grandfather were also named Walter, in memory of his enslaved ancestors, who were forced to accept names given by their owners.

Beach told Stern he did not wish to be "named," and that he felt an imposed nickname was a vestige of slavery. A few weeks later, Beach received in the interoffice mail, a nameplate from Stern with the nickname "Cornerback." Beach felt the name had a racial connotation, and he refused to wear it. In subsequent meetings, Beach says he felt a "chill" from Stern.

Beach saw a pattern of preferential treatment for whites in promotions within Brooklyn for supervisory jobs; he expressed his view of unfair treatment to the chief of the department's EEOC office in a written memo, in August 1998. He never received a written or verbal reply to his formal complaint.

In December 1998, Beach assigned a black woman to be the manager of the Metropolitan Avenue pool in

Williamsburg. This was the first time that Beach assigned a person of color to a supervisory job in a mostly white neighborhood.

The Parks Department bosses rejected this black woman and said they would conduct their own interviews for the position. For years Beach has filled managerial jobs in black neighborhoods without any interference from higher authorities.

Beach then wrote a memo saying three blacks he had recommended for promotions were being rejected because of "bias."

At this point, Walter Beach was fired. And the job at the Metropolitan Avenue pool was given to a white employee.

In the federal EEOC complaint, the "forced resignation" of Beach was listed as "an act of discrimination and retaliation."

Paula Loving started working at the Parks Department in the Work Experience Program, while Dinkins was still mayor. Then, under Stern, she saw two younger white women promoted above her. These jobs were never posted, and there was no interviewing process in which Loving could establish her qualifications.

Angelo Colon stared working at parks in 1988, rising to the job of recreation center manager. Then he applied for the position as Manhattan coordinator of pools, a job with a higher salary. But Stern gave it to a younger white subordinate whom Colon had trained. Colon then watched his trainee be promoted to be the deputy chief of recreation in Manhattan. When Colon applied for the same job again, it was given to a younger white woman.

Robert Wright worked at parks since 1979. He has considerable experience coordinating youth and recreational programs throughout New York City. He was finally offered, under Stern, the position of managing the Asser Levy Recreation Center on East 24th Street—one of the city's premiere recreation centers and a traditional stepping-stone to better jobs in the department.

But this offer was mysteriously rescinded by Stern's aides, who told Wright he had a choice of being transferred to one of four recreation centers, all in black or Latino neighborhoods.

A white woman who had not even applied for the job was then given the plum assignment to manage the Asser Levy Center.

The EEOC complaint was drafted by Lewis Steel, one of New York's best civil-rights lawyers, who had won high-profile police-brutality and employment-discrimination cases over the last thirty-five years.

When Steel filed this complaint in 1999, he told me, "Rudy Giuliani is responsible for this. He created the climate for this kind of discrimination by throwing out the affirmative-action plan that was in place under Dinkins. Giuliani's plan was so watered down that it was meaningless. This sent a message to commissioners like Stern that City Hall would turn a blind eye towards discriminatory promotions and hiring at city agencies."

Steel also pointed out:

> The Parks Department had an excellent black commissioner, Gordon Davis, under Koch in the late 1970s. Davis hired blacks and Latinos at the deputy commissioner and assistant commissioner level. The department was integrated at the management level twenty years ago. But eventually these minority managers moved on or retired. And Stern did not replace them. Today there is not one black among the top twenty-five executives and managers in the department. And I can tell you that if this case gets to trial, we will prove that Henry Stern uttered racial slurs . . .
>
> Stern says that two of the top thirty managers are Hispanic. But when we did some research, we discovered that one of those he counted as Hispanic had one grandfather from Spain, and three white grandfathers. And this guy couldn't speak a word of Spanish.

After almost three years of depositions and briefs, the Justice Department stepped in and sued Stern and the Parks Department for racial discrimination in June 2002.

The federal government's lawsuit accused the Parks Department of favoring whites in promotions—especially those who were part of a special program created by Stern to attract graduates of elite colleges, called the "Class Of" program.

The Bush Justice Department found the Parks Department failed to follow any objective guidelines for deciding who to promote to management jobs, failed to post notifications of management job opening, and "rarely, if ever," conducted the required interviews for vacancies.

The suit accused Stern of not only failing to promote qualified blacks and Latinos, but of seeking out and promoting whites without even conducting formal interviews. Stern ran an affirmative-action program for white people, giving them extravagant preference.

In announcing the lawsuit, United State Attorney for the Southern District James Comey said, "Employees have a fundamental right of equal opportunity in the public workplace. We are filing this case to vindicate this right."

Part of the Justice Department's case rests on Stern's "Class Of" program. The government concluded that this program was really a device to allow whites from Harvard, Yale, and Princeton to leapfrog to management jobs over equally, or more qualified, blacks and Latinos, who did have seniority and experience, but not Ivy League pedigrees.

The suit described the "Class Of" program as "disproportionately white and non-Hispanic." And as "a separate promotional track for white participants." Stern had claimed that the "Class Of" program was one-third minority.

The government's suit says the discrimination goes back to 1995, and seeks back pay and other forms of relief for all the victims of discrimination. A trial, and a separate class-action lawsuit, are both pending in the federal courts in Manhattan.

The federal government's lawsuit emphasized the discrimination suffered by Robert Wright, who was the lead plaintiff in the original EEOC complaint.

On the day of his vindication, Wright was asked about all those white kids from Princeton and Dartmouth who were jumped over him in pay and promotions.

"I have nothing against these young people," Wright, now forty-seven, replied. "But I had to earn my stripes and move up the ladder. What we have found is that for us, the ladder is sixteen feet tall, but for them it is only eight feet tall."

Early in 2001, the EEOC had issued a ruling saying there was reason to believe the complaint filed in 1999 had merit, and that parks employees had been denied advancement because of their race. At that point, there were some improvements in the Parks Department, and Wright was promoted to be the manager for parks in Harlem.

But on the day of his vindication by the federal government, Wright said, "I felt I was ready to work on this level a long time ago."

Perhaps the weirdest and most self-defeating consequence of Giuliani's racial view of the world was his refusal to even meet with most elected black leaders of the city. He just ostracized and ignored them. Most of the time, nobody noticed. But whenever there was a crisis between the police and the black community, this childish boycott became a public issue. The mayor gave various reasons for his personal avoidance of cross-racial dialogue.

For years he did not meet with State comptroller Carl McCall, Harlem Congressman Charles Rangel, or Manhattan Borough President Virginia Fields. Queens Congressman Gregory Meeks told me he did not have one conversation, even on the phone, with Giuliani in eight years. McCall told me that Giuliani ignored his requests for a meeting for five years. When Fields asked that lines of communication be opened, he ridiculed her and claimed she applied a "race overlay" to too many issues.

When tensions were high after the police killed unarmed African immigrant Amadou Diallo in 1999, McCall says he had "one meeting for show" with Giuliani, but promises of continuing conversation with a substantive policy agenda were never kept. Giuliani also held one meeting with Fields, and one with Bronx Borough President Fernando Ferrer. And then went back to silence and shunning.

In December 2000, Giuliani was asked to explain his policy of not speaking to elected legislators representing black communities in the traditional, retrospective yearend interviews with City Hall reporters. The mayor, feeling righteous in his decision to treat black leaders like Ralph Ellison's *The Invisible Man,* said he was able to "do more to help" minority communities by ignoring their elected leaders. He insisted he did not regret having no relationships with black leaders.

"If you engage in dialogue with political leaders that pander, you end up watering down change so much, that nothing changes," he said. He did not mention white politicians who pander—a prevalent species.

He also justified his boycott approach by claiming that many black politicians advocate "a philosophy of dependence" that has kept black communities "enslaved." (You can't make this stuff up—it's so bizarre. For more details, see David Seifman's article in the December 29, 2000 *New York Post*, under the headline: RUDY: BLACKS BEST WITH MY NO-TALK STYLE.)

In 1999 I had a private dinner with Giuliani, and attempted, in a nonconfrontational way, to understand Giuliani's thinking behind his refusal to meet with moderate, elected blacks. He offered several rationales, none of which made much sense.

He claimed he treated black and white exactly the same and tried not to have "a separate relationship with the separate communities."

Treating everyone the same sounds well-intentioned and high-minded. But, in theory it pretends that everyone is exactly the same. It pretends that racism doesn't exist, that class and cultural differences don't exist, that the needs of millionaires and immigrants are the same.

Giuliani, in practice, did treat communities differently. The more they voted for him—Queens, Staten Island,

Jews, Italians—the better he treated them. He named Bruce Teitelbaum to be his liaison to the Orthodox Jewish community. If there was a local problem with the trash, or a traffic light, or police ticketing, Teitelbaum was called and the problem got expedited attention.

There is nothing inherently wrong with this. But there was no equivalent liaison with the city's black communities. If there is equal access to a City Hall insider by each ethnic, religious, and racial group, that's fine, and it's the way it was under mayors going back to John Lindsay in the 1960s.

But under Giuliani, communities like Harlem and Bed-Stuy had no institutionalized access to City Hall, while other communities, with less severe problems, had greater access.

Giuliani kept repeating to me that blacks are essentially the same as whites, and didn't need any individualized consideration, access, or sensitivity.

This seemed an absurd premise in a city where the NYPD too often profiled, stopped, and frisked young black and Latino males without reasonable suspicion.[2]

And in a city where poverty and unemployment

[2]In December 1999, State Attorney General Eliot Spitzer issued a 178-page study of racial profiling by the NYPD. Analyzing 175,000 "stop and frisk" reports, Spitzer found that Latinos were stopped 39 percent more often than whites, and blacks 23 percent more often. Spitzer found that 15 percent of all the searches of minorities did not meet the legal standard for "reasonable suspicion." And 25 percent of the reports did not contain enough information to be interpreted.

among blacks and Latinos was twice as high as among whites.

And in a city where schools, housing and hospitals in black and Latino communities were inferior to those in white communities.

Spitzer also did a separate analysis of stops by the Street Crime Unit (SCU), four of whose members has killed Amadou Diallo as he reached for his wallet on the doorstep of his own home. The Attorney General found that 23 *percent* of the stops made by the SCU were unconstitutional.

The SCU stopped 16.3 percent blacks for every stop that led to an arrest, compared to 14.5 percent for Latinos, and 9.6 percent for whites.

The Spitzer study concluded that "even accounting for the fact the minority neighborhoods have a higher crime rate, blacks and Hispanics were still more likely than whites to be stopped by police."

Giuliani also rejected the idea that slavery was a singular and exceptional historical experience—much like America itself. He said he did not believe that slavery still had psychological and sociological implications for the black family structure, for policy makers thinking about day care, or welfare reform, or creating housing to keep homeless families intact.

I came away from this evening reluctantly thinking that this man I had known for fifteen years, who had shown no bias as U.S. Attorney, who had campaigned as a liberal on homelessness and inclusion in 1989, now just did not feel human empathy for black people.

I now felt the worm of rancor was eating away at his heart, a heart that seemed to be shaped like a clenched fist.

It is true that many blacks will never forgive Giuliani for defeating Dinkins, their champion and symbol of pride. But as the mayor of the most racially diverse city on earth, Giuliani had a higher moral and legal obligation to be forgiving.

He was mayor of the whole city, and had a responsibility to rise above his private anger and resentments, and govern from higher ground.

To some extent, his views on race were probably opportunistic. His political house was white. After two bitter campaigns against Dinkins, he was never going to get much black support. So he pandered to his base.

Some of the most revealing conversations Rudy Giuliani had about race came with two of his closest black supporters—former Queens Congressman Reverend Floyd Flake, and his own deputy mayor, Rudy Washington, a Queens Republican.

In the midst of racial tensions surrounding the killing of Diallo and Giuliani's defensive, pro-police responses, Reverend Flake and Giuliani met at the Fame Diner in Queens. Rudy Washington arranged the meeting and attended it. Flake had endorsed Giuliani in 1997 against Ruth Messinger. He was even considering joining the Republican Party and was a star speaker at Republican gatherings.

Flake arrived, upset by the Diallo killing, and by the racial profiling and harassment of black teenagers by the police, especially the profiling of the middle-class children of his church parishioners. Flake was expressing the emotions of having dignity and rights violated, describing specific injustices he knew to be true.

Giuliani responded with statistics, impersonal, boilerplate data. So Flake decided to share with him a personal narrative about what happened to him a year earlier, when he was still a member of Congress. Flake recalled how he was driving with his wife to his church at night, and how his car was stopped by a white police officer.

"Nigger, didn't I tell you to stop that car?" Flake quoted the cop as yelling at him.

After realizing he had pulled over a congressman, the officer let Flake go. But Flake wondered what would have happened if he had not been a member of Congress.

Flake could see that his humiliating personal experience, which burned his soul, was making no impact on the mayor. In the mayor's closed mind, statistics were trumping reality.

Flake looked at the mayor and told him, "You've got a mean streak in you."

This meeting ended Flake's friendship and political alliance with Giuliani. Later Flake told Giuliani biographer Andrew Kirtzman: "Anyone who disagrees with him is treated almost as a personal enemy. He treats everything as if it's a urinating contest."

In the same period, right after the Diallo killing, Deputy Mayor Rudy Washington had his own intimate conversation with Giuliani. He recounted two demeaning experiences when he was stopped by white police officers for no good legal reason—while deputy mayor—and treated disrespectfully.

In the second incident of profiling, a young white officer pulled Washington over, told him to get out of his car, and asked for his ID.

Washington handed him an ID that identified him as a board member of the MTA, the state authority that managed the city's trains and buses.

The cop thought it was a fake ID. He pushed Washington against his car and told him he was taking him down to the police precinct to check his ID.

At that point Washington's wife, Deborah, began to cry.

As the cops prepared to place Washington in a squad car, their commanding officer, a lieutenant, pulled up and recognized Washington.

The lieutenant took the paperwork and gave it back to Washington. Giuliani's response to this painful memory from the only black among his senior staff was to continue to deny that racial profiling existed in the NYPD. But he arranged to give Washington a special police identification badge with his name on it. Washington was instructed to keep this badge with him at all times, in case he was stopped again for no reason.

This was an individual solution that exempted one middle-class, middle-aged black man from a policy that afflicted the rest of his race in Giuliani's New York.

Early in 2002, Ray Kelly, the new police commissioner, banned all racial profiling in an official, written communication sent to all of the city's police precincts and commands.

In an interview, Kelly told me:

> We will not tolerate racial profiling. It's against the principles of this country. I think we are the only police agency in the country that abolished it as a practice and policy.
>
> I believe that ending racial profiling has made a contribution to the improvement of race relations in the city. You have to put some goodwill in the bank, so that when a sudden crisis comes, people will give the benfit of the doubt, you have some credibility in the community.

Meanwhile, New York's new mayor, Michael Bloomberg, has met with all of the city's elected black and Latino leaders within two months of his inauguration. He shunned nobody. He talked to Rangel, Ferrer, McCall, and Meeks. He had Bill Lynch and union leader Dennis Rivera to his home for dinner. He spoke regularly and productively with the new black comptroller, William Thompson. He was the guest at a reception hosted by the council of Elected Black Democrats. With his police commissioner, he even paid a visit to Al Sharpton's headquarters on Martin Luther King's birthday.

Bloomberg had more contact with the black community in eight weeks than Giuliani had in eight years.

Just by being inclusive, open, and not emotionally embattled, Bloomberg created a better atmosphere of cooperation between the mayor's office and the black community.

Today in New York, there is visibly less racial tension. It's harder to start a racial squabble now. The city's long racial fever seems to have broken, at least for now.

Some of this is directly attributable to the more mellow mood after 9/11. There is now a greater sense of unity and community in the city, more of a sense of civic patriotism, and fatalism. Knowing death so well, we New Yorkers now have a sense of proportion about life.

But some of this new mood is also caused by the absence of Giuliani. The leader of the city is no longer in our living rooms, shunning, profiling, and insulting one portion of the city's people.

5.
Louima, Diallo, and Dorismond

On March 26, 1998, I was astonished by Rudy Giuliani at a time when I thought nothing he did could surprise me anymore.

I was at City Hall for his press conference to release a report on the NYPD that had been commissioned by Giuliani after cops at the 70th Precinct in Brooklyn had sodomized and tortured an innocent thirty-year-old Haitian immigrant named Abner Louima in August 1997.

The barbarism suffered by Louima had occurred during the mayor's re-election campaign. He responded the way a mayor should. He visited Louima in the hospital. He called the beating "reprehensible." He transferred the top commanders of the 70th Precinct in a public rebuke for the breakdown in discipline. And he quickly formed this high-level commission that contained some of his toughest critics, like Norman Siegal of the NYCLU, and some of his closest allies, like Staten Island Borough President Guy Molinari, and solid law-enforcement professionals, like former police commissioner

Robert McGuire, and Thomas Reppetto, the director of the Citizens Crime Commission.

Giuliani knew how one racial crime could transform a New York City election. He saw how the murder of Yusef Hawkins by a white mob in Brooklyn had helped David Dinkins defeat Ed Koch in the 1989 Democratic primary. He understood that Dinkins's passivity during two nights of rioting in Crown Heights in August 1991 had shifted enough Jewish voters to his side in 1993 to give him a narrow victory over Dinkins.

So he did all the right things when Louima was victimized in a police-station bathroom by sadistic cops. Norman Siegal called Giuliani's immediate response "his best 48 hours as mayor."

This is why Giuliani's press conference, releasing his own commission's report, was so disturbing and mystifying. He dumped all over the report, insulting his friends who drafted it.

Giuliani's comments at the press conference were sneering and sarcastic. His words dripped with derision and disdain.

"Some of the things we've already done," he told a room packed with reporters and TV cameras. "Some of the things I've opposed in the past, and I'll continue to oppose them. And some of the things are unrealistic, and make very little sense."

Mockingly, he referred to the most trivial of the more than seventy-five specific recommendations—one that suggested changing the title of the NYPD's deputy commissioner for community affairs to deputy commissioner for community relations.

"I think that's Recommendation 9B," Giuliani said with a smirk. "That's a good change. We can change it from affairs to relations."

Giuliani never mentioned any of the report's constructive proposals. Higher pay for police officers. More minority hiring and diversity. An expansion of the police-cadet program. Better psychological screening in hiring. Sensitivity training taught to new recruits in the police academy. A greater emphasis on courtesy in dealing with the public. Designating community-patrol specialists in each precinct, instead of rotating them out to other assignments. Weeding out the wackos after the training period. Requiring new hires to live inside New York City. These all made obvious sense.

The task force report made the essential point that cops and civil liberties are not zero-sum rivals. There is no reason why society can't have *both* less crime and less police brutality. Cops can be aggressive and heroic without being belligerent or racist. There is no inherent contradiction between good policing and liberty.

The members of the commission, who had labored for seven months, were appalled at the snub. "I'm just flabbergasted," said Abe Foxman, the director of the Anti-Defamation League of B'nai B'rith.

Reverend Michael Faulkner, a pro-Giuliani black minister told me, "The people of the city, and the NYPD, are the losers when our report is not taken seriously. You have busy people, who poured their heart and soul into this process, attending dozens of meetings. This was the most diverse task force in the history of New York City. And today I feel like our work was not taken seriously."

Christine Quinn (now a member of the City Council) said, "If it was so off base, so ludicrous, why didn't the mayor intervene and tell his staff to guide us? The mayor assigned eleven staff members to work with us, and they never said anything to suggest our thinking was going in the wrong direction. The mayor disrespected us. The majority report was substantive and constructive."

(There was a more radical minority report, signed by the NYCLU's Norman Siegal and three members of the thirty-two-member task force. The dissenting report urged the appointment of a special prosecutor for police brutality and corruption.)

At the close of Giuliani's press conference, I asked one of his City Hall staff members to tell me, in confidence, what triggered the mayor's disowning of such a mainstream report signed by his appointees and friends.

"The pay raise for the police freaked him out," I was told.

The next day I asked my close friend Eric Breindel, the conservative editorial-page editor of the *New York Post*, and a commission member, to explain what I saw.

"I can't explain it," Breindel, who was exceptionally close to Giuliani, admitted. "It made no sense. The report is a sound piece of work. I signed it."

My best guess now is that the commission itself was

just a transient ploy to get through the election of 1997. Even though Giuliani was outspending Democrat Ruth Messinger by $10 million to $3 million, he was in campaign mode when he assembled the commission in response to what was done to Abner Louima.

In March 1998, the campaign was over, Giuliani was re-elected with 58 percent of the vote, and these consensus reforms irritated him.

His sarcasm was not diluted by the fact that his own close friends like Breindel, Molinari, and Robert McGuire affixed their names and reputations to the proposals.

Giuliani never even met with the task force to thank them for their efforts. Or to follow up on their recommendations. Or refine them into something better.

He just made them invisible in his mind.

Giuliani was probably never serious about addressing the causes of the Louima tragedy once the election was over. Or about improving relations between the police and the city's communities of color. He may have wanted only a public-relations kind of report that stressed the NYPD's successes.

Giuliani was infuriated by the recommendation of a salary increase for the police—then in the third year of a five-year labor contract. This eruption highlighted one of Giuliani's most fundamental contradictions. He would mount knee-jerk defenses of the police in almost any circumstance, but he would not give them the pay increase they so plainly deserved. The cops were keeping crime down below the national average, and this was keeping

Giuliani popular, but he would not reward their high-risk performance.

This caused the further contradiction of Giuliani wrapping himself in the aura of the NYPD, while many rank-and-file cops disliked him over wage and union-contract issues, despite his defense of them in each controversial shooting or beating incident—except for Louima.

One cop told me, "I'd rather get more money than the benefit of the doubt."

Four 70th Precinct police officers were eventually convicted for their complicity in the sodomizing of Louima, and the city paid Louima a large civil settlement for his injuries and degradation.

The police brutality visited upon Louima was the first of three horrific police episodes that occurred in New York City during Giuliani's second term. The other two were the deaths of unarmed Amadou Diallo, who was shot forty-one times and killed by police on his doorstep. And unarmed Patrick Dorismond, who was killed in a struggle with undercover narcotics cops after he rejected their request to buy drugs from him. He died saying no to drugs.

The question is this: Could the deaths of Diallo and Dorismond have been made less likely if the reform proposals made by the Louima task force had been implemented?

Would better training have made a difference? Would a more integrated police force have made a difference?

Would a message from City Hall that there was no longer any presumption the police were right in all questionable shootings have made a difference? Would a public embrace of the ideas of the task force have created more restraint and accountability?

What was done to Abner Louima, inside a police station, should have been a "red flag" to Giuliani that something had gone haywire inside the city's police culture.

Four white police officers felt immune to arrest and openly committed crimes against Louima inside their precinct, feeling no need for secrecy or discretion. They acted as if they were guards in one of Pinochet's jails in Chile. Justin Volpe shoved a broom handle up Louima's rectum, and then jammed the stick into his captive's mouth. Louima's small intestine was punctured, his bladder badly damaged, and he had to be given a colostomy bag.

Louima had done nothing to justify an arrest, much less this torture. There was a fight outside a nightclub, somebody in the crowd had sucker punched Volpe, and Volpe mistakenly arrested the innocent Louima for assault and disorderly conduct.

At trial, Volpe's lawyer claimed Louima had suffered his injuries during gay sex. Only late in the trial, with the evidence piling up against him, did Volpe abruptly plead guilty.

This should have been the fire bell in the night, a warning that some cops were psychos out of control, dangers to the public safety and order they were sworn to protect.

But Giuliani ridiculed the report of his own task force, that proposed dozens of ideas for incremental reforms of police hiring, training, procedure, and deployment.

This denial—this refusal to hear the fire bell—was the wrong mistake, at the wrong time, in the history of New York City.

The minority community was angry about racial profiling. Black leaders were sick of being shunned. The Civilian Complaint Review Board was getting increasing numbers of allegations of police misconduct and brutality. Anthony Baez had been choked to death in the Bronx in 1994 by police officer Francis Livotti, who eventually went to prison for violating Baez's civil rights. At the same time, cops were sometimes falsely accused of brutality by drug dealers, and were bitter about not getting the raises they deserved in the good times economy of the late 1990s.

The tension was combustible; Giuliani should have defused it in 1998.

The task force report on police/community relations was another lost opportunity, a potential opening for reconciliation, ruined by that deep reservoir of anger that Rudy Crew had experienced and named.

Amadou Diallo was a hardworking immigrant from West Africa, living in a small apartment with three roommates at 1157 Wheeler Avenue in the Bronx. He sold videos on 14th Street in Manhattan and returned home at about midnight on February 4, 1999.

He was a devout Muslim who prayed five times each day. He had no criminal record. He did not own a weapon. He had a work ethic. He was the model of the striving immigrant who made New York City what it is.

Diallo was standing on the doorstep of his home when four white cops from the aggressive, elite Street Crime Unit noticed him from their unmarked police car.

The four young cops—Edward McMellon, Kenneth Boss, Richard Murphy, and Sean Carroll—all wearing bulletproof vests, stopped their car and got out to approach Diallo.

According to the trial testimony, McMellon said, "Please show me your hands."

It is not known if Diallo understood what he was saying.

Diallo reached for his wallet, perhaps to show the cops his identity.

"Gun!" Carroll screamed.

The four cops fired forty-one shots in seven seconds, nineteen of them striking Diallo and killing him.

All the assumptions and perceptions of these four young cops were wrong on a dark Bronx street that night.

They thought Diallo was a criminal, but he was not.

They thought he was reaching for a gun, but he was not.

They thought he resembled the sketch of a rape suspect, but he did not.

They thought he was an intruder, but he was not. Cops have to make split-second decisions under pressure—and these were all bad.

It is inconceivable to me that if Diallo were an unarmed white man, standing in front of his own home, in a middle-class white neighborhood, that the police would have fired once at him, much less forty-one rounds.

All four officers belonged to the Street Crime Unit, which was already a big problem to police critics, but a problem that might have been repaired by some of the proposals made by the Louima task force that Giuliani dismissed eleven months earlier.

Only 3 percent of the 400 cops in the Street Crime Unit were black. Police Commissioner Howard Safir had tripled the size of the unit when he replaced William Bratton because the unit had been effective at taking guns off the street.

But Safir expanded the SCU without adequate specialized training or psychological screening. Anybody could volunteer and get into the unit, whose bravado motto was "We own the night." It attracted the most hyperaggressive young cops, who were inexperienced.

Richard Savage quit as the commander of the SCU because he believed the rapid expansion without the proper controls was a blunder.

The SCU cops shaped up each night at Randall's Island and went to a different unfamiliar minority neighborhood. They could not distinguish between the drug dealers and the dedicated, lawful workers like Diallo. They were an inexperienced occupying force that was virtually all white. They had discretion without supervision.

In 1997 and 1998, the SCU stopped and searched 45,000 people, and made only 9,500 arrests. Its arrest numbers were dwindling, while its stop-and-frisk numbers were rising—proof of diminishing returns on an obsolete strategy.

The future police commissioner—Ray Kelly—would disband the Street Crime Unit and retire its tainted name from use early in 2002.

As the lifeblood ebbed out of Diallo in his small vestibule, Sean Carroll took his victim's hand and said, "Please don't die! Keep breathing!"

But other members of the SCU then ransacked Diallo's apartment, looking for anything that might incriminate him. They upended beds, dumped his clothes on the floor, tore the drapes from his bedroom window. They searched for evidence against the victim, not the perps.

His roommates were taken to the 43rd Precinct and interrogated for more than six hours. They were not told that Diallo had been killed by other police officers.

His roommate and cousin, Abdourahamane Diallo, told columnist Jim Dwyer, "They wanted to know did he have enemies, was there anyone who could have done such a terrible thing."

Dwyer wrote that the police pulled records to see if Diallo had a criminal history, or if any narcotics arrests had been made at 1157 Wheeler Avenue.

They could find no blemish in Diallo's background; the justification for such an inquiry into Diallo's life is hard to imagine, except to dirty him up, to make his killing seem less heinous, less senseless, less reckless.

Dwyer reported that all five cops who searched Diallo's tiny apartment were white, and in plainclothes.

When the facts of the shooting became known to the whole city the next day, there was almost unanimous outrage: forty-one shots, no gun, no criminal record, his own doorstep, reaching for a wallet.

Giuliani behaved the way any mayor should—at first. He offered to pay the plane fare for Diallo's father to come to New York from Vietnam. Five days after the killing, he told reporters, "My heart goes out to them. No one wants to lose a child, and the idea of even talking to the father, and talking to him about losing a son in a foreign country, is a terrible, terrible thing."

When Diallo's beautiful and almost regal mother, Kadiatou Diallo, arrived from Guinea in West Africa, Giuliani did try to meet with her and offer his condolences.

But by then, Reverend Al Sharpton had entered the picture and made a quick connection with the mother, while the mayor's office tried to work through the divorced and less forceful father.

Sharpton was able to prevent Giuliani from meeting with Diallo's mother, through the interposition of allies with whom the mother felt more comfortable.

Giuliani was trying to be sympathetic, but his years of hostility and exclusion directed at the black community could not be overcome in this crisis. Giuliani had no friends in the city's black leadership he could turn to now.

He had lost the trust of anyone who mattered. He had no contacts, no back channels, no brokers. His chickens were coming home to roost. He had isolated himself from a large portion of the city.

A few months later, Reverend Al Sharpton gave me a candid account of how his maneuverings kept Giuliani from meeting with Diallo's family. It shows how treacherously politicized the nexus of cops and race had become in Giuliani's New York. Sharpton said:

> Rudy came to the Rihga Royal Hotel, thinking he was going to meet with Diallo's parents. But I didn't want him to co-opt the parents for his own purposes. So he ended up waiting for an hour and never seeing them. . . .
>
> Rudy didn't understand the situation. The parents were divorced and hostile to each other. Rudy tried to work through the father, but we had the mother, who was a lot smarter.
>
> Rudy had nobody around him who had any credibility in the black community. Nobody trusted him because of all the awful things he had done the previous years. You were there. You saw what happened at the funeral at the Islamic Center. Rudy got booed and heckled by the mourners. His security detail had to shield him. He couldn't cope with the whole situation.

For about two weeks, Giuliani seemed to grasp the

intensity of emotion in the city over the Diallo killing. He was on his best behavior, as he was after the torture of Abner Louima.

But he couldn't submerge his anger or his defensiveness about the police, or his loathing of his critics in the black community and the press very long. He didn't know how to leave bad enough alone. And neither did his police commissioner, Howard Safir.

In late February Safir was interviewed by Dominic Carter, a workhorse on NY1, the all-news cable station. As Safir was walking down a corridor, Carter was asking him questions about the racial composition of the Street Crime Unit.

Carter asked the commissioner whether the public had a right to know more about the unit that had been responsible for Diallo's death.

"I've told you twenty times," an angry Safir said, with the tape in the camera rolling, "the Street Crime Unit is overwhelmingly Caucasian. We do not keep a count by racial background or ethnicity. You've been told this twenty times and you keep asking the question over and over, for whatever racial reason *you* might have. But it's not for the public."

Dominic Carter is a black professional journalist with no racial agenda or bias. He was doing his job. And Safir was not.

Safir was attributing a racial motive to Carter, when it was Safir who had the racial attitude. Safir looked at Carter and saw race, the way the cops looked at Diallo and saw race.

On Tuesday, March 9, Reverend Sharpton began leading nonviolent civil-disobedience protests over the killing of Diallo, and over the fact that the four officers had not yet been indicted.

At first these demonstrations were relatively small and received only scattered media coverage. Their hard core were radical and nationalistic activists who followed Sharpton's media-centric leadership.

These protests included ugly, provocative signs equating Giuliani with Hitler, and the NYPD with the KKK. Giuliani responded with some nasty remarks of his own.

On March 11, Harlem Congressman Charles Rangel called Sharpton and told him he wanted to get arrested the following Monday. Rangel had seen Giuliani demean the Diallo protests on television and was incited to direct action. With almost thirty years of seniority in Congress, and a secure power base in Harlem, Rangel was a force. Other politicians respected his intelligence, and his keen sense of strategy and timing.

A few days later, former Mayor David Dinkins advised Sharpton that he, too, would submit to arrest on March 15, outside the headquarters of the New York City Police Department, behind City Hall, at One Police Plaza. Then Queens Congressman Gregory Meeks volunteered to join them.

At the appointed hour, hundreds of people, led by the former mayor and the two congressmen, sat down in the street in front of police headquarters. For a while the police on duty declined to arrest them.

Finally, the graying, dignified ex-mayor of the city and the two congressmen entered the NYPD's headquarters building, where they were placed under arrest.

Dozens of television cameras and photographers were there to record this extraordinary event that had its roots in the civil-rights and anti-apartheid movements.

The next day, the picture of Dinkins getting arrested was on the front page of the *New York Times*—above the fold—the message to the city, and to the rest of the media, that this was history in the making. The TV news-assignment editors take their cues from the placement of stories in the *Times*.

Giuliani, who had two bitter elections against Dinkins, overreacted. He attacked the media and, by implication, Dinkins, and the *Times*.

"This is a great publicity stunt," Giuliani said. "Can't you figure it out? It's a publicity stunt, and you are, as usual, sucked into it."

He called the protests "silly."

Giuliani had lost sight that this was about Diallo—and not about him. It was about justice, about whether New York's legal system could be fair to a dead immigrant from West Africa.

Over the next two weeks, more than 500 New Yorkers went down to police headquarters to get arrested. Movie stars like Susan Sarandon, Ossie Davis, and Ruby Dee. State Comptroller Carl McCall. Bronx Borough President Fernando Ferrer. Union leaders. NAACP president Kweisi Mfume. Ruth Messinger, who lost to Giuliani in 1997.

Rabbis and ministers. City Council members. Even little old ladies who *liked* the police were getting arrested.

On March 16, the *New York Times* published a poll that disclosed that Giuliani's job-approval rating had plummeted to *42 percent*. This was down 21 points in five months. A majority of the city was against him now, including many whites.

In reacting to the poll results, Giuliani said the leaders of the demonstrations were "partisan and inaccurate." He also blamed a "media frenzy" for distorting reality, and affecting public opinion.

The poll also showed that less than 25 percent of all New Yorkers thought the police treat blacks and whites in an equal and fair manner. Almost 90 percent of New York's black residents believed that the police often engage in brutality against blacks.

Giuliani quoted accurate statistics that showed that the NYPD had killed ninteen civilians in 1998, compared with forty-one in 1990, when Dinkins was the mayor.

But the perception of a mean, blindly pro-police Giuliani had reached a critical mass with the public. What they saw him saying on television was consolidating their opinions. The data wasn't penetrating their awareness.

This same perception problem had once haunted Dinkins when he was mayor. Crime had gone down in 1992 and 1993, but the impression of rampant, violent crime had sunk in through television coverage in 1990. The average person remembered the high-profile homicides, their own feelings of fear, and the Crown Heights rioting of 1991. They didn't notice the slight improve-ment reported in small stories in the newspapers, as the crack epidemic slowly began to recede.

The City Council scheduled a public hearing on the Diallo killing and the police, for March 28. They invited Police Commissioner Safir to testify, but he declined, citing a "scheduling conflict."

The night before the hearings, the Academy Awards were presented in Hollywood. And a television camera happened to catch Safir in a tuxedo, striding down the red carpet, shaking hands with the stars.

The tape played all over the local TV news shows and did not make the police commissioner look good. It looked as if he was setting a callous tone to a grieving community. It made him look as if he was snubbing the City Council to party with the celebrities.

The backlash was so intense that Safir had to take the red-eye flight back and show up at the City Council.

And it later turned out that he had gotten a free trip to Los Angeles and had to reimburse the corporation that flew him out there.

In yet another tone-deaf act of insensitivity, Giuliani defended Safir's junket.

"Frankly, there is no crisis or emergency going on, and things have been proceeding quite normally," he said.

This was out of sync with what most of the city was feeling. The remarks further angered not only the black and immigrant communities, but many middle-class and working-class whites.

On April 4, I was at City Hall covering Giuliani. By then almost 1,000 people had been arrested at the daily, disciplined protests at police headquarters. There had been no violence.

When he was asked about the protests, Giuliani complained they were being fueled by "obsessive media concern."

Then he refused to answer three more questions about Diallo.

"Why don't we talk about something else today?" he said with his best sneer of disgust.

"Why don't we *not* get back to the police issue?" he said. "Why don't we, on this day, actually be disciplined enough to talk about something else. There are other things that affect life in this city."

Virtually every reporter attending this daily press availability found his remarks disturbing. And he was certainly misguided in his complaint that the Diallo killing was being overplayed because of some obsession unique to the media and not shared by the public. People were talking about it—at the office, in the park, at the bar. The story warranted all the attention it was getting.

On March 31, the four cops were indicted by a Bronx grand jury. The next day, Giuliani went to the Bronx and spoke to about 100 police officers gathered to honor a fellow officer killed in the line of duty. In this emotional tinderbox, Giuliani chose to attack the critics of the police in the Diallo case.

The police, he declared, are "being second-guessed by some of the worst in society."

To some, this sounded like a reference to Dinkins, Ossie Davis, and Susan Sarandon.

In Andrew Kirtzman's excellent book, *Rudy Giuliani: Emperor of the City,* there is a killer anecdote from this period, set on April 11.

Because so many of Giuliani's friends were unhappy with his handling of the Diallo killing, Giuliani agreed to sit behind a two-way mirror with his pollster, Frank Luntz, and listen to a focus group talk about their perceptions of him. The focus group consisted only of white New York residents.

These white New Yorkers were saying Giuliani was not sensitive enough in his responses to the Diallo shooting. They felt he was not apologetic enough. They wanted the mayor to express compassion for Diallo and his family, without reverting to his ritualistic defense of the police.

When the focus group ended, Kirtzman described how Giuliani turned on his pollster, Frank Luntz, who idolized Giuliani.

"This was a waste of time," Giuliani yelled. "I've learned nothing from this! I am not going to give in to the mob mentality!"

Giuliani was furious at Luntz, and at all his other advisers who were asking him to be a little kinder, a little more empathetic.

"I'd rather not be mayor than do something unprincipled,"

a red-faced Giuliani screamed at Luntz and his other silent advisers.

One mark of a great leader is the capacity to be objective about yourself. Guiliani does not have this quality. He couldn't admit a mistake. He couldn't see himself the way others see him. He couldn't listen to a different point of view. He was a prosecutor, an advocate with a made-up mind.

It remains a great regret that Giuliani could not rise to this occasion, after Diallo's death, the way he did when the two hijacked planes turned the Trade Center towers into crematoriums for 2,800 people.

If Giuliani had been able to make objective decisions, if he had been eloquent, caring, reassuring, and unifying, the way he was on 9/11, then the city would have been spared much rancor and division.

But he just didn't have it in him.

The goal of the Diallo protest movement had been justice, equal justice under the rule of law. But they didn't get it. The four officers indicted for the shooting were all acquitted—but by a jury of people living in Albany, not the Bronx, where the shooting took place.

One of the cops—Sean Carroll—hired as his lawyer Burton Roberts, the former administrative judge of the Bronx, and the former district attorney of the Bronx. Roberts knew everybody in the game.

After the case had been assigned to Patricia Williams, a capable black trial judge in the Bronx, Roberts made a change of venue motion to the appellate court. He had been elected by the people of the Bronx, but he wouldn't let his client be judged by the people of the Bronx.

In December 1999, five white appellate judges ruled the trial had to be moved to Albany, where there is not a single black judge. The judges decided the four cops could not receive a fair trial from the citizens of the Bronx, who happened to be about 80 percent black and Latino.

In dozens of other cases, judges have ruled against a change of venue motion in cases with even more prejudicial pretrial publicity than this one. The Islamic terrorists who bombed the World Trade Center in 1993 were tried in Manhattan. John Gotti's change of venue motion was rejected. Justin Volpe, who had tortured Abner Louima, had his change of venue motion turned down. He was convicted in Brooklyn.

The Albany trial was assigned to Judge Joseph Teresi, who had presided mostly over civil trials. Judge Williams of the Bronx was a former prosecutor with criminal-trial experience.

The change of venue ruling rigged the game, and slanted the playing field.

Even before the trial started, Judge Teresi made an absurd ruling on a pretrial motion. He ruled inadmissible the evidence that two of the four officers had proven citizen complaints against them for misconduct in their records, after hearings before the Civilian Complaint Review Board. They had a history of violent overreactions.

In most trials I have covered, relevant past similar acts were ruled admissible as evidence. Judge Williams of the Bronx might have allowed the jury to know there had been past founded complaints in the record.

In his instructions to the jury, Judge Teresi said the use of deadly force could be found justified if the cops believed Diallo was a robber—although no evidence was ever presented that Diallo was a thief or intruder.

Judge Teresi's charge gave the jurors the rationalization that the shooting was self-defense, even though Diallo was unarmed. The judge was transporting the jury into the imaginations of the defendants, but *not* into the skin of the victim.

All four cops were acquitted. Considering the evidence the jury was allowed to hear, it is hard to call their verdict a total miscarriage of justice. The cops did not set out to kill anybody that night. There was no criminal intent. It was a tragic, miserable mistake. The cops did not have the proper training, or supervision, and they panicked.

The day after the verdict, I published a column saying that I would have voted to convict Officers Carroll and McMellon of reckless endangerment because they fired first and emptied their weapons. And I would have voted to acquit Officers Boss and Murphy because they fired second, and mistakenly thought some of the ricocheting bullets were coming from Diallo.

The change of venue ruling by the all-white appellate panel was worse than the jury's decision. It helped to determine the outcome. So did Judge Teresi's unfair charge to the jury.

The strategy of the defense was to get the case away from a black judge and a Bronx jury. And they did it.

None of this was Rudy Giuliani's fault or responsibility. But the result added to the existing feeling that many New Yorkers had, that the criminal-justice system was not evenhanded, that blacks did not always receive equal justice under the rule of law.

And in this climate, on March 16, three weeks after the acquittal of the Diallo cops, there was yet another horrendous police killing of an unarmed, innocent black man.

Patrick Dorismond was a twenty-six-year-old Haitian immigrant employed as a security guard by the 34th Street Partnership, working the 3 P.M. to 11 P.M. shift.

After work he visited the Wakamba cocktail lounge with Kevin Kaiser, a coworker. The bar was located in a run-down area near the Port Authority bus terminal, where there was a lot of drug dealing, addicts, homeless people, prostitutes, and teenage runaways.

When Dorismond and his friend left the bar, they stood along Eighth Avenue, trying to hail taxicabs. That's when Dorismond was accosted by an undercover narcotics cop named Anderson Moran. Moran asked Dorismond if he wanted to sell drugs to him.

Officer Moran had no reasonable suspicion or probable cause to approach Dorismond. Dorismond was not acting suspiciously. He did not have any drugs on him. He did not have any bulge in his clothing that might indicate a gun.

He was not a vagrant. He was not loitering. He was not trespassing. There was no legal reason to approach him.

If Patrick Dorismond were white, he would never have been asked for drugs by the police.

Police Officer Moran was part of a new NYPD initiative called Operation Condor. Condor was part of Giuliani and Safir's "zero-tolerance" policy for pot smoking, loitering, trespassing, and other "quality of life" misdemeanors.

"Zero tolerance" was a bastardization of the "broken windows" theory of policing. But it became more aggressive and interventionist, leading to more interactions with citizens and to stop-and-frisks of minorities. "Broken windows" was about cops using discretion to deter disorder that might breed crime, like outdoor drinking out of paper bags, or a loud radio being played late at night by rowdy teenagers. It focused on residential neighborhoods, not Times Square.

The "broken windows" theory gave the police a choice of sanctions. They might give an informal warning to a homeless man urinating in public, or they might arrest a fare beater. What they did was usually popular with the local population; it deterred crime and quieted annoying behavior.

George Kelling, the co-creator of the "broken windows" concept with James Q. Wilson, has said, "Zero tolerance is a phrase I never use, never have used. It is antithetical to what I'm talking about."

The fatal flaw in the "zero tolerance" Operation

Condor was that it was not enforced equally across the city. It focused on the poor, and on the areas where they congregated.

There were no plainclothes Operation Condor cops in the upscale bars around Wall Street, where stockbrokers in suits and suspenders sometimes made cocaine purchases.

There was no Operation Condor deployment in Battery Park, or the South Street Seaport, where young lawyers and bond traders sometimes smoked pot. No Armani suit was patted down; no Lexus was searched.

Operation Condor was an example of the arbitrary and discriminatory enforcement of misdemeanor laws.

Marijuana arrests around the bus terminal rarely took any guns off the street, or led to busting any major drug gangs for felonies. They certainly didn't help reduce the homicide rate.

"Zero tolerance" was a publicity concept, applied unequally to the rich and poor. It was also the theory that propelled Officer Moran to ask Patrick Dorismond for drugs, one night on Eighth Avenue, near Times Square.

Dorismond was insulted and got into a fight with Moran. The backup team arrived, and in the melee, Dorismond was shot and killed. A grand jury voted not to indict any of the officers.

The weeks following Dorismond's death were the lowest ebb of Giuliani's mayoralty. He went on another Venom Binge of excess.

In an effort to discredit the victim before his funeral, Giuliani instructed his police commissioner to make public Dorismond's *sealed* juvenile-arrest record, without getting a court order. This was an *arrest* record—not a criminal record of adjudicated crimes.

There was nothing in the arrest record punishable by anything more serious than a summons. There was nothing nearly as serious as the *adult* criminal record of Giuliani's own father, who served sixteen months in Sing Sing Prison for armed robbery before Giuliani was born.[3]

Then the mayor went on Fox-TV and declared that Dorismond "was no altar boy."

But, in fact, Dorismond *had* been an altar boy. And he had gone to Bishop Loughlin—the same Catholic high school as Giuliani. But this common root generated no sympathy or identification.

Giuliani also released the autopsy report on Dorismond which found a trace of marijuana in his system. But toxicology experts said the trace was so negligible that it could have come from inhaling secondhand smoke from someone else's smoking a joint. I then visited the Wakamba bar and could smell pot in the air. Jimmy Breslin also visited the bar, and also inhaled the sweet aroma of weed.

[3]Barrett's book quotes from a presentencing psychiatrist's report on Giuliani's father: "He is egocentric to an extent where he has failed to consider the feelings and rights of others."

The next day Breslin wrote an inspired column for *Newsday*. It concluded:

"Giuliani's acts of indecency put much more of a strain on the reeling woman who was Dorismond's mother.

"In all the years, of all the cheap politicians of this city, nobody in record or lore has ever gone lower or lousier than Giuliani."

When a reporter asked Giuliani a question about Dorismond's having been an altar boy, the mayor refused to answer it on the grounds the reporter was being "argumentative," as if he were a judge ruling a lawyer's question inadmissible.

When he was pressed about releasing the sealed juvenile-court record, Giuliani argued that since Dorismond was now dead, he no longer had any privacy rights. The only lawyer in the city who agreed with Giuliani on this point was his own corporation counsel.

Such a rampage of meanness towards a dead man, killed by the police for saying no to drugs, drove a whole segment of the city away from Giuliani, in a recoil of revulsion.

An early April poll published in the *Times* revealed that 79 percent of city respondents believed that Giuliani's comments on the shooting "made the situation worse." And 60 percent of suburbanites shared this opinion. Moderate and independent voters were cringing at his cruelty.

The same poll disclosed that Giuliani was suddenly trailing Hillary Clinton, 49-to-41. Two months earlier, Giuliani had been ahead, 46-to-41. His indecent attacks had caused a sea change in the electorate.

In the middle of Giuliani's campaign of vilification against Dorismond, I paid a visit to Reverend Michael Faulkner, to write a column about the minister who had started a prayer fast to "convince Giuliani to either have a religious conversion or resign."

Faulkner had been a strong supporter of Giuliani, one of the few black clergymen to endorse Giuliani against Dinkins in 1993. Giuliani had appointed him to his post-Louima police task force, and to a Charter Revision Commission. In his younger days Faulkner had also played one season of professional football with the Jets.

Faulkner had served an apprenticeship to Reverend Jerry Falwell at Liberty Baptist College, and was occasionally seen on local television defending the mayor.

He had first felt "some disenchantment," when Giuliani mocked the reform recommendations of the Louima task force. But it was the release of Dorismond's sealed juvenile record that broke it for Faulkner.

"The immorality of what the mayor did superseded the illegality of it," Faulkner told me.

I pointed out to Faulkner that Giuliani had recently been saying of anyone who criticized his conduct, that they "are reading from Al Sharpton's script."

"He can't do that to me. I'm reading from God's script."

Reverend Faulkner then returned to his feelings about the police/community task force report being ridiculed and rejected.

"Rudy was wrong," Faulkner said. "You always affirm and appreciate volunteers. We put blood, sweat and tears into that report. And he discarded our opinions and efforts.

"He didn't like the fact we urged higher pay for the police, so he blew off our report. I'm a spiritual leader. I know that how you treat people is what you get back. If you treat people like crap, they will treat you the same way."

I asked Faulkner what he was praying for during his fast, which was then in its tenth day.

"I'm praying for the mayor to have a change of heart," he replied. "Rudy is my friend, but he has become an obstruction to justice."

A few days later, a writer for *The New Yorker* magazine asked Giuliani whether he had any second thoughts about releasing Dorismond's sealed records.

This was Giuliani's answer:

"I read the law myself. The law contains no prohibition against releasing records if someone is dead. It doesn't speak to the subject, and therefore it leaves, even granting the other side as much leeway as possible, an ambiguity.

"If the state legislature wanted to create a protection beyond death, they should have written it into the law. So legally I don't have any reconsideration."

With the exception of Hillary Clinton and Ruth Messinger—both of whom he was running against—Rudy Giuliani's most excessive Venom Binges were directed against people of color.

Patrick Dorismond. Rudy Crew. Ramon Cortines. The

leaders of the Diallo protest movement. And the artist who offended him the most, and triggered his assault on the Brooklyn Museum and the First Amendment—an African named Chris Ofili.

6.
The Opportunist

During the 1960s, Rudy Giuliani was a self-described "Robert Kennedy Democrat."

When he was a student at Manhattan College (1961–1965), he wrote an article for the campus newspaper supporting RFK over Republican Kenneth Keating in the 1964 Senate election. Peter King recalled him being sympathetic to the black rioters of Newark and Detroit during 1967.

During the liberal 1960s, Giuliani was definitely liberal.

But in 1975 Giuliani switched his party registration from Democrat to Independent, just before he got a job in Gerald Ford's Justice Department, according to his mentor, Harold "Ace" Tyler. Tyler is the former federal judge who hired Giuliani as his deputy, to help him run the criminal division of the Justice Department in 1975.

On December 8, 1980, Giuliani changed his party registration again. This time he shifted it from Independent to Republican. This was just one month after Ronald Reagan's election, and just as Rudy was applying for a job to be the assistant Deputy Attorney General of the United States. He got the job under William French Smith. Three years later, President Reagan appointed Giuliani to be the United States Attorney for the Southern District of New York.

In the conservative 1980s, Giuliani was becoming conservative or perhaps he was only a chameleon, taking on the coloration of a conservative.

He even fooled his own mother. In an unpublished interview, Helen Giuliani said of her son, "He only became a Republican after he began to get all those jobs from them. He's definitely not a conservative Republican. He thinks he is, but he isn't. He still feels very sorry for the poor."[4]

The timing of these two changes of party loyalty give off the odor of opportunism. A cunning and audacious opportunism is probably the most consistent thread running through Giuliani's career.

The most articulate formulation of this view comes from former Bronx Borough President Fernando Ferrer, who served in that office during all of Giuliani's tenure as mayor. Ferrer observed him close up. Ferrer was also the only mayoral candidate in 2001 who refused to go along with Giuliani's demand for three extra months in power, which were not provided for in either the City Charter or the term-limits law.

[4]This interview was conducted in 1988 for a biography of Giuliani that was never published. It was later quoted by Wayne Barrett in his Giuliani biography, published in 2000.

Rudy is all about opportunism and utility. I do not think he is a racist at all. In a way, he is something worse. A racist can't help himself. It's the way he is. But the opportunist can help himself, and chooses not to. The opportunist engages in discrimination or stereotyping out of a calculation that it is profitable in some way. There is some cynicism involved.

It's all about power with Rudy. He only believes himself, not in any large ideas. His core value is loyalty to *him*. That's why he is always surrounded by the loyal group. Rudy will say anything, or do anything, to win, to get his way. There is no underlying belief system.

Everyone's personality is an onion with many layers. I believe that opportunism is the core of Rudy's onion, after you peel away all the other layers.

In 1989 Rudy Giuliani ran for mayor as a crusader for the more humane treatment of the homeless. He promised to build more housing for the homeless and to create a system of smaller, less Dickensian shelters. He took an intense tutorial on the issue from lawyer Bob Hayes, then the director of the Coalition for the Homeless. They spent three full days together, touring shelters and discussing what they saw. Rudy was trying to position himself as more liberal on this issue than the incumbent mayor, Ed Koch, who he thought would be his opponent in the general election.

On May 17, 1989, Giuliani formally announced his candidacy for mayor. This is what he said that day:

"Homelessness is not a matter merely of statistics and economics, it is a matter of conscience.

"Each time the administration attacks those less fortunate, by exaggerated and cruel characterizations, New York loses a bit of its soul."

A few weeks later, Giuliani released a specific eleven-page program, detailing what he would do to help the homeless. It was more liberal, more compassionate, and more ambitious than anything David Dinkins, or the other three Democrats running for mayor were proposing. Giuliani promised to open emergency shelters for homeless families and single adults. He ridiculed the Koch administration for doing nothing, and forcing homeless advocates to sue in court.

Giuliani asked in one speech, "What kind of leadership leaves the governing of our city to the courts? Common decency, conscience, and commitment compels us to do better."

As a candidate Giuliani emphasized the homeless issue, casting it in moral terms.

What he said, day after day, was virtually the same thing that Bob Hayes and the Coalition for the Homeless had been saying for years, as they litigated against the

Koch administration to provide better services, better health care, and more housing.

Giuliani lost the 1989 election to David Dinkins. He tried again in 1993, and early in the campaign, he was still echoing Bob Hayes, Mary Brosnahan, and the Coalition for the Homeless.

Then, suddenly late in the campaign, he changed his position; he began attacking the right to shelter. Overnight he started to sound like the Manhattan Institute, the conservative think tank which had also been tutoring him in issues like homelessness, welfare, and education. They gave Giuliani a way of looking at poverty through a filter of "a culture of dependency," and fiscal tough love.

By the summer of 1993, the public mood had shifted after a series of assaults by homeless men. The problem had gotten worse after all the years of liberal compassion. Dinkins had fumbled around with the issue and never developed an effective policy.

This social problem was more intractable and complex than anyone thought—including the advocates for the homeless. The solution wasn't just, "housing, housing, housing," as Bob Hayes once said.

When Andrew Cuomo started HELP, his own non-profit organization, he made a survey of single homeless adults in the Fort Washington shelter. He found that about 70 percent of them had disabling underlying maladies of substance abuse, alcoholism, or mental illness. There had to be social services to also address these afflictions.

There had to be transitional housing to teach the homeless daily living skills. There had to be the job training and drug counseling. There had to be work-ready skills, and day care, and parenting skills.

Cuomo pointed the way towards a holistic social-service strategy, towards the goal of a "continuum of care" and new housing, to make a difference. This helped educate advocates, reporters, and liberal, sentimental politicians, on how hard it was going to be to lift people out of homelessness, and back into productive society.

This complexity, this lack of easy progress, led to frustration, and to compassion fatigue among the electorate. A few horrific crimes committed by homeless men hardened some attitudes.

In the autumn of 1993, Rudy Giuliani and his campaign team detected this change in public opinion and decided to use it to their political advantage. This dwindling of civic sympathy for the homeless also coincided with the harsh ideas Giuliani was picking up from the conservative academics at the Manhattan Institute.

Homelessness was no longer "a matter of conscience" to Giuliani. It was now a matter of convenience, of campaign tactics. He met with Andrew Cuomo, but did not adopt his modified, unsentimental liberal approach. He went all the way over to the Manhattan Institute's punitive approach, based on saving money.

With Bob Hayes in 1989, Giuliani talked directly to homeless people. In 1993 at the Manhattan Institute, he talked to academics and theoreticians.

This time Giuliani wasn't running against Ed Koch from the left. There was little political reward in sounding compassionate about the homeless in a campaign against an incumbent black mayor, who already had the backing of most unions, most liberals, and almost all blacks. Giuliani's growth potential was to his political right, among voters who saw the homeless as beggars, vagrants, crazies, and criminals.

By 1993 Mary Brosnahan had replaced Bob Hayes as the director of the Coalition for the Homeless, although she had been there in 1989 and seen Giuliani tour the shelters, ask questions, read materials, bond with Bob Hayes, and say all the right words. Brosnahan told me in September 2002:

Early in the 1993 campaign I still had hopes for Giuliani. I felt he had been sincere in 1989. Dinkins was not good on the issue-he built no housing, he reduced funding, families were sleeping on the floors of the Emergency Assistance Unit in the Bronx, and not getting placed in shelters. We were unhappy with Dinkins. He was a C-minus mayor in terms of the homeless. But he wasn't mean-spirited, or contemptuous of the poor.

Then one day I got a call from the *New York Times* reporter Celia Dugger. She told me Giuliani was going to attack the right to shelter the next day. We had no warning this was going to happen. We were stunned. We showed up the

> next day and denounced Giuliani's change of
> position at his own press conference. It was
> just cold opportunism. There was a growing
> frustration in the city, and he decided to
> take advantage of it, and betray the homeless,
> and abandon us.

Late in the 1993 election, Giuliani made public his new position on the homeless. He said that residents of the shelter system would no longer be in the pipeline for subsidized permanent housing. He was joining Dinkins in the belief that some families "made themselves homeless," in order get on a preferred list for subsidized apartments—although no one was able to prove this cynical theory was true.

Giuliani also said he would place a ninety-day limit on shelter stays by families; that they would have to find their own housing by this arbitrary deadline, even in cases of domestic violence or arson.

Candidate Giuliani also said that if elected, he would ask the state legislature to overturn state-court orders and judicial-consent decrees, signed by previous mayors, that codified the right to shelter, and promised assistance in finding permanent housing.

Giuliani was vowing to reverse the court orders won by Bob Hayes, the activist lawyer who gave him his education about homeless people four years earlier, and who had guided him through the worst of the shelters on nighttime tours of misery.

Guiliani defeated Dinkins by 50,000 votes to become

mayor. In the final analysis, his abandonment of his homeless advocacy was probably not a major factor in his narrow victory.

A referendum on secession from New York City, which was on the ballot on Staten Island, motivated a larger-than-normal voter turnout in the most conservative borough, adding thousands of extra votes to Giuliani's total. Dinkins's failure to stop the rioting in Crown Heights for two nights in 1991 shifted thousands of Jewish votes to Giuliani. The black turnout was down in 1993, compared to what it was in 1989—about 1,500 fewer voters in each of the black assembly districts.

According to the television exit polls, 85 percent of Giuliani's vote was white, 9 percent Hispanic, and 3 percent black.

Giuliani's conversion stands as one small proof for the proposition that opportunism illuminates his public life—like a neon through line.

Giuliani's first year as mayor was ideologically ambiguous, a season of mixed messages. Late that October of 1994, Giuliani endorsed liberal Democrat Mario Cuomo for governor, rather than moderate Republican George Pataki.

But even this act of political courage and independence may have had an opportunistic origin. Cuomo told me, "Rudy endorsed me because somebody showed him a poll that said I was going to win. I think that's why he did it, in all honesty."

By the summer of 1996, Giuliani began to enforce policies harmful to the homeless. He began replacing social workers at the intake centers with "fraud investigators."

According to Patrick Markee, senior staff analyst at the Coalition for the Homeless:

> The rejections of applications for beds in shelters went from 800 in 1995, to 11,000 in 1996. Rudy began to erect impediments to shelter. The Emergency Assistance Unit, where homeless people went for emergency housing or a shelter assignment, became his laboratory. He set up a system of barriers designed to discourage homeless people from applying for shelter. He created hardships as a way to reduce demand.
>
> At the same time, he was cutting the funding for housing in the capital budget. This was the great lost opportunity in 1996 to 1999, when the economy and Wall Street were booming. When the city had a budget surplus. He could have built some affordable housing in these good times.
>
> Mayor Koch had allocated about $5.2 billion to rehabilitate or construct 150,000 units of housing. Ten percent of these apartments went to the homeless. These apartments were in Harlem, the South Bronx, and Brooklyn. Rudy could have done the same thing, but didn't.

In October 1999, Giuliani launched a new offensive

against the homeless. He said the police would arrest any homeless person who refused shelter, even though many homeless people felt the city's shelters were unsafe bedlams of violence.

Giuliani's homeless policy had come down to an absurd contradiction. His administration was going into court to bar some people from entering the shelter system and erecting barriers to shelters while, at the same time, the mayor was instructing the police to arrest homeless people on the street if they refused to go to a shelter. He was also sending the police into the shelters to arrest people under outstanding misdemeanor warrants.

The homeless were being shuttled back and forth like cattle, in a bureaucratic maze bereft of sensitivity, individuality, or rationality.

Mary Brosnahan says, "By the end of 1996, we had no access to Giuliani. We were put on his enemies list, along with the Legal Aid Society and Housing Works [the militant AIDS advocacy group]. He stopped all funding for the Coalition for the Homeless. He deleted $2 million from the budget to fund our SROs in Manhattan. Rudy's people at City Hall started smearing us, telling nonprofits and service providers not to even meet with us. He tried to punish us for disagreeing with him."

The homeless problem continued to deteriorate during Giuliani's second term. There was a famine of housing for the poor. Rents kept rising. Then, when the economy began to slow, and then tank, unemployment increased. Then with the attack on the World Trade

Center, about 25,000 low-wage jobs in lower Manhattan were destroyed—in hotels, and restaurants and garment shops in Chinatown. And then unemployment insurance benefits began to run out after 26 weeks.

In 1998, there were 21,000 homeless people in New York City. By the fall of 2002, there were 36,000—a *70 percent* increase over four years.

Patrick Markee told me that 20 percent of the homeless who passed through the Coalition's offices actually had part-time, or off-the-books jobs, and still could not afford to pay rent.

Sometime during his second term, according to several of his former commissioners, Giuliani came to the settled point of view that "people could just will themselves out of poverty."

He came to accept the early-twentieth-century Darwinian idea that there were "deserving poor," but also "undeserving poor." He saw all jobless adults without drug or drinking problems, without mental or physical handicaps, as slothful malingerers, looking to rip off the system.

Giuliani believed that any poor person could wake up one day and just decide they didn't want to be poor anymore, and get a job if they really wanted to—even when the New York City unemployment rate was hovering around 8 percent.

Shortly before Christmas 1999, Giuliani said he was going to require all ablebodied homeless people to work for their shelter—an extension of his policy requiring all welfare recipients to work for their benefits.

This new Giuliani edict would only drive more homeless people into the streets, just as the cold winter weather arrived. A *Times* editorial called it "unduly punitive to the most down and out residents of the city. . . . Most New Yorkers support the idea of requiring welfare recipients to work in exchange for benefits. But even supporters of workfare are startled by a plan that might force homeless people back into the streets."

At a pre-Christmas rally in Union Square of 1,000 people against Giuliani's plan, Reverend Al Sharpton shouted:

> If you look at Mary's story, if Mary had lived in Bethlehem under Mayor Giuliani, they would have given Jesus to a foster-care program.
>
> If Jason Turner [Giuliani's commissioner in charge of welfare policy] had come into the barn that night, he would have said to the baby Jesus: "You have been born to two unwedded parents. They don't have an address. They don't have a job. We have to take you into custody and arrest your parents."
>
> It's legal to camp out for Yankees tickets, but not if you are poor.

Giuliani quietly pulled back from this plan that would have flooded the frozen streets with more men sleeping in cardboard boxes, and starting fires for warmth in garbage cans.

The distinction between Giuliani and his 1960s hero,

Robert Kennedy, must be defined sharply here. RFK, whom Giuliani often quoted during his liberal 1989 campaign, also disliked the dependency he saw that a welfare check and idleness bred in its long-term recipients.

But RFK also hated poverty. He crusaded for free food stamps to combat hunger and malnutrition in children. He fought for an expanded government role in the creation of jobs, and for higher minimum wage, for more funding for education, from prekindergarten to adult literacy, more job training programs, and more day care funding, so mothers could look for work without worrying about the safety of their children.

"Jobs, not welfare," was RFK's stump-speech slogan, all through his 1968 campaign for president. He believed that work conferred self-respect, confidence, and dignity. But he also understood that you could not just will yourself out of poverty or unemployment.[5]

One final judgment on Giuliani's homeless policy

[5]Giuliani's workfare program was more mixed than his homeless policy. New York's welfare rolls did fall from 1.1 million in 1996 to 450,000 during the summer of 2002. This helped the budget and led some people to steady work.

But the "one shoe fits all" policy also had a punishing aspect. The Human Resources Administration did delay benefits if an applicant missed one appointment, and did discourage people from applying for food stamps. In May 2002, Mayor Bloomberg changed some of Giuliani's policies, saying that "education and training should count as work." And that some families should be exempted from the federal five-year limit on welfare benefits. Bloomberg has a more flexible approach, moving away from Giuliani's rigid "workfare or nothing" concept.

was passed in the courtroom of Judge Helen Freedman on September 19, 2002. That's when the Bloomberg administration ended years of litigation by agreeing to pay back fines to thousands of homeless families who had to sleep on the floors and desks of city offices, when the city could not find them a room to sleep in between 1995 and 2001.

The settlement, negotiated with Steven Banks of the Legal Aid Society, will cost the city about $10 million, for indignities inflicted by the Giuliani administration.

Judge Freedman, who presided over the settlement, had sometimes been personally attacked by Giuliani, for being a dupe of homeless advocates. All the litigation over the right to shelter had been in her jurisdiction through four consecutive mayors.

The Giuliani administration had litigated for six years out of a stubborn adherence to ideology. The Bloomberg administration applied a balanced impulse to be decent to the homeless, and get rid of a nagging lawsuit.

This was the day I went back and reread Giuliani's campaign speech from 1989, in which he attacked Koch. He declared:

"What kind of leadership leaves the governing of our city to the courts? Common decency, conscience, and commitment compels us to do better."

Rudy Giuliani's fiscal opportunism caused New York City to go from a $3 billion budget surplus in 1998, to a $4.5 billion budget deficit when Giuliani left office on

December 31, 2001, that grew quickly to $5 billion, by November of 2002, for fiscal year 2003–4.

This mismanagement of prosperity is a large part of the Giuliani legacy. He left the city's finances in a mess that was aggravated by the recession, and the collateral damage to the city's economy from 9/11, including unexpected expenditures for cleanup, overtime, and relief.

Giuliani spent his surplus in two ways. First on projects he thought would help him in his anticipated Senate campaign in 2000 against Hillary Clinton. And then on polishing his legacy in his final year, after he pulled out of the Senate race.

In an interview in August 2002, City Comptroller, William Thompson, told me:

"I would estimate that about $2.5 billion of the city's $5 billion budget deficit in fiscal 2002 was attributable to Giuliani. He rolled over the debt each year and funded the projects and programs he thought would benefit him politically."

Giuliani bequeathed his successor a huge budget deficit by increasing spending by more than 5 percent during his second term, which was twice the rate of inflation; by adding 25,000 people to the city's payroll—many of them patronage hires; by increasing debt payments to $4 billion a year; by using fiscal tricks that pushed the costs onto future generations; and by enacting tax cuts of $2.2 billion that mainly benefited the wealthy.

State Comptroller Carl McCall issued a series of public reports during 2001 that gave Giuliani fair warning that he was making a long-term mistake, for the sake of short-term popularity.

On May 17, 2001, McCall predicted a budget gap of almost $4 billion for the fiscal year that would begin on July 1, 2002. This was when Giuliani was still claiming the city had a surplus.

McCall's fiscal analysis concluded: "It's clear that tough times are ahead. It's inexcusable for the City to be in this position after a string of record surpluses. But rather than put the surpluses toward paying down the debt, and building up reserves, the city chose to use them to balance the budget one year at a time. In that sense, what we're seeing isn't a surprise. It just should never have come to this."

McCall pointed out that the city's debt-service costs are projected to consume almost 19 percent of tax revenues by the 2005 fiscal year, compared to less than 16 percent in the present fiscal year.

On July 11, 2001—pre-9/11—McCall released another warning that Giuliani was mismanaging the city's golden years. The state comptroller's report said:

> As I've said time and again, the most respon-
> sible use of these record surpluses of the
> past few years would have been to reduce the
> city's mounting debt burden, and build a
> reserve fund for that rainy day that will
> inevitably come. Instead, on the heels of
> unprecedented prosperity, the city faces the

> prospect of service cuts. That's simply
> inexcusable.
>
> The record budget surpluses of the past few
> years afforded the city a golden opportunity
> to get on the path toward long term fiscal
> stability. The opportunity has been squan-
> dered.

One of those who criticized Giuliani on his borrowing habits during a boom period was the conservative Tom Carroll, the president of Change New York. In the February 21, 2001 issue of the *New York Times*, Carroll was quoted saying of both Giuliani and Governor George Pataki:

"There wasn't the fiscal discipline we had hoped to see overall. But on the debt, there was no discipline at all."

On the day Giuliani left office, the city's workforce was the highest in history—tens of thousands more than when Giuliani came into office, promising to reduce the workforce.

One place where Giuliani did not spend his surplus was on workers or union contracts. Labor lawyer Basil Paterson, who represents municipal unions with 175,000 city employees, told me:

> Giuliani did *not* do what Governor Pataki did,
> which was spend some of the surplus on labor
> contracts. Pataki did this for hospital workers
> and teachers. Giuliani just refused-for more

> than a year-to even negotiate with the teachers
> and the police unions. What he did was repre-
> hensible. He spent the surplus on everything
> but the workforce. I think he resented the work-
> force.
>
> Rudy knew he was term limited. But he chose
> to leave Bloomberg, whom he endorsed, with
> this huge deficit. The last time this was done
> was 1965, when Mayor Wagner left John Lindsay
> with a deficit, and no money to pay for labor
> contracts. This is what really caused the
> transit strike on Lindsay's first day in
> office.

During Giuliani's term as mayor, the city's debt rose by more than half, by about *$15 billion.*

This is why Giuliani's fiscal monitors, on both the Left and the Right, agree that the good times were paid for partly with borrowed money.

The irony is that Giuliani was actually a profligate spender—but without targeting the spending towards the poor and most needy.

If a liberal Democrat had borrowed with such abandon, and had so quickly converted a surplus into a deficit, the bond raters and editorial writers would have caricatured him as a drunken sailor on a binge. Giuliani was hardly scolded at all. McCall's earnest reports didn't even make it into most newspapers.

In June 2002, Mayor Bloomberg had no choice but

cobble together a budget with gimmicks that postponed the day of fiscal reckoning for a year.

New York City will now have to face a growing $5 billion budget deficit in the fiscal year that begins on July 1, 2003. Bloomberg had to borrow $1.5 billion just for operating expenses for this fiscal year.

The city's economic future is now in history's pawnshop, because of Giuliani's ambition-driven, and legacy-driven spending and borrowing between 1999 and 2001. Bloomberg now has to *both* raise taxes and cut services in 2003 to balance the leaking budget that Giuliani left him.

There are dozens of other examples of Giuliani's uninhibited opportunism.

In the chapter on the schools, I have already told the story of how his sudden change of heart on school vouchers cost him a capable schools chancellor and destabilized the city's education system. For years Giuliani attacked the idea of vouchers in an unprompted fashion in speeches, saying they violated the constitutional separation of church and state. But as soon as he started planning a campaign for the Senate, he switched his view to reposition himself more favorably with Catholic voters outside the city.

As a candidate for mayor in 1989, Giuliani mounted a moral crusade against political patronage. He saw it—correctly—as the underlying root cause of the corruption of the Koch administration that he had prosecuted successfully as U.S. Attorney. He understood that Democratic Party clubhouse bosses, like Donald Manes, Stanley

Friedman, and Meade Esposito, had placed corrupt individuals like Geoffrey Lindenauer and Alex Leiberman on the city payroll, in order for them to rig contracts, fix bids, and extort kickbacks.

Candidate Giuliani promised "to make certain the corrupting influence of patronage is removed from government once and for all. There will be no patronage in my administration."

But there were thousands of patronage hires in Giuliani's administration. Many of the 25,000 people he added to the city's payroll came from political leaders allied with Giuliani. Agencies like the Housing Authority and the Department of General Services became notorious as patronage dumping grounds. He installed a patronage dispenser right in City Hall—Tony Carbonetti—later promoting him to chief of staff. Carbonetti's father had been a friend of Giuliani's father.

It was only after Giuliani left office that his broken promise of no patronage ripened into a scandal, thanks to a remarkable series of articles by Tom Robbins in the *Village Voice*.

Ray Harding, the boss of the Liberal Party, emerged as a major lobbyist in the city under Giuliani—because he had given Giuliani the Liberal Party line on the ballot in 1989, 1993, and 1997. Harding himself filled hundreds of patronage slots on the city payroll with Liberal Party members, and his family members. By 1996, 145 city employees were members of the minuscule Liberal Party, which was not liberal at all, using the name as a fraudulent label.

One of those hires was Russell Harding, who became

the president of the New York City Housing Development
Corporation, a self-financing public-benefit corporation.
Russell Harding was a college dropout with no experience
in housing, and zero qualifications for the job. Ray
Harding's other son—Robert—became Giuliani's budget
director, on the merits.

While Giuliani was still mayor, Tom Robbins submitted a Freedom of Information request to examine Russell Harding's expense records. He was told he was not
entitled to see them, and besides, they could not be
found—probably lost.

But when Michael Bloomberg became mayor, the
records were located quickly and provided to Robbins.
The result was a series of articles—and a criminal investi-
gation by the U.S. Attorney.

It turned out that Harding put in for—and received
reimbursement for—about $250,000 in improper travel
and entertainment expenses. These included all-expense-
paid trips, with luxury accommodations, to Las Vegas,
Hong Kong, and San Diego—for Harding and a close
friend. He even billed the taxpayers $1.25 every morning
for his bagel. Russell Harding was a patronage parasite.
He would never have gotten his job—from a mayor who
promised to eliminate patronage—if his father hadn't
been such a patronage pipeline and power broker.

Do not get me wrong. I am not saying that Giuliani is
some unique or extreme mutation among politicians
when it comes to chameleon-ism. Most politicians—

certainly, most triumphant politicians—are equally as opportunistic as Giuliani.

Think of Bill Clinton. Think of George Bush, Al Gore, Joe Lieberman, Robert Torricelli, and Alfonse D'Amato.

Think of Hubert Humphrey, Richard Nixon, George Wallace, Dan Quayle, and Lyndon Johnson, who promised America "no wider war" in his 1964 re-election campaign.

Most politicians are guided by constant polling and focus groups. The few exceptions are those who know who they are and have a principled philosophy: Jim Jeffords, Ted Kennedy, John McCain, George McGovern, Mario Cuomo, Phil Hart, Jim Jeffords, and Paul Wellstone.

McGovern, a World War II bombing hero, opposed the Vietnam War when only 20 percent of the country agreed with him. Mario Cuomo vetoed death-penalty legislation eleven times, knowing that only 25 percent of the voters agreed with him.

But the preponderance of politicians will abandon any position that is unpopular, and say whatever will help them win the next election. Most of them are slaves to fashion and popular passion.

There is just one thing that is different about Rudy Giuliani. It is that he has now acquired a reputation for high and consistent principle—while still possessing his highly developed opportunistic dexterity.

Rudy is good at it because he has the capacity to convince himself of the purity of his own rectitude—no matter what he is doing.

7.
The Power Play to Stay

Poor man wanna be rich,
rich man wanna be king,
a king ain't satisfied till he rules everything.

—Bruce Springsteen, "Badlands"

The unrestrained adulation rained down on Rudy Giuliani in the days following his performance on September 11, 2001. The city and the world celebrated his serene leadership in the face of mass murder and potential hysteria. His energy, eloquence, and organizational skills filled a void left by weaker leaders.

He received standing ovations when he walked into ballparks and restaurants. It was almost a folk-hero phenomenon. People greeted him with the chant, "Rudy! Rudy! USA! USA!" He was Charles Lindbergh and Davy Crockett rolled into one.

Very quickly this adulation began to convert itself into a movement for Giuliani to remain the mayor. It was a movement he nourished in private, as his aides like Joe

Lhota and Robert Harding assured him that he was indispensable to the city's unity and renewal.

But the sneak assault of the terrorists had come on an election day, at a time when Giuliani could not remain the mayor of New York under existing law. The law and the election cycle would have to be tampered with if Giuliani were to continue to be the mayor. And Giuliani was not prepared to bow gracefully and exit the stage with the applause ringing in his ears.

On September 21 posters began to appear on walls and lampposts all over the city, proclaiming: "Giuliani for Mayor. Paid for by Grateful Citizens of New York City."

They sprouted on the block where I live in Greenwich Village. They were in every borough. Somebody was spending a lot of money to jump start a popular uprising against the term-limits law. It was monarchy disguised as populism.

Also on September 21, the *New York Post* ran an editorial urging that Giuliani remain in office "for as long as it takes to get the job done." The editorial proposed postponing the election.

The voters had approved term limits in two referendums, and Giuliani's term was over at the close of 2001. The attack came on the morning of the primary elections to choose Giuliani's successor. When the towers fell, the voting was halted and the primary rescheduled for September 25.

Giuliani could get another term as mayor only if the state legislature voted to repeal the term-limits law. This statute covered the three citywide elected officials, the five borough presidents, and the entire City Council. But Giuliani and his advisers were talking about repealing the term-limits law only for Giuliani—not for the rest of the government.

Giuliani was trying to ignite a Giuliani Forever movement without looking power crazy.

For a few days, the city was filled with rumor and speculation about Giuliani's intentions, about whether he was even willing to stay on. On September 25—primary day—he told reporters that he was "available." That night he told Dan Rather in a CBS-TV network interview, "I am open to the idea of doing it," making it sound like a draft.

John Faso, the Republican minority leader of the state assembly, immediately announced he would introduce legislation allowing Giuliani to remain in power. Governor Pataki said, "Whatever the mayor's decision is, I will support that decision."

Then Mike Long, the leader of the anti-choice Conservative Party, offered to give the pro-choice Giuliani his party's line on the November ballot. Long said the party's nominee, Terry Gray, would gladly withdraw in behalf of Giuliani.

Business leaders began to burn up the phone lines trying to generate support for Giuliani remaining as the mayor. The buzzword was "unity."

Even Sheldon Silver, the Democratic speaker of the assembly, said he would raise the possibility with his party conference—although he was personally opposed to the idea.

Giuliani and Governor Pataki held a series of phone

conversations on how this might be accomplished legally, without a court fight. It would be a delicate dance in the middle of an ongoing election.

The behind-the-scenes maneuvering drew in Stanley Michels, a liberal Democrat on the City Council, who opposed term limits, and was leaving office at the end of the year because of term limits.

"I got a call on my cell phone from Deputy Mayor Joe Lhota," Michels told me in an interview for this book.

> Lhota asked me to come immediately to his office. When I got there, Lhota asked me to introduce a new bill into the City Council-under my name-to repeal term limits just for Giuliani. He said it did not have to pass, or even come up for a vote. Lhota told me he had reason to believe that if I did this-and it had to be me-then the governor would postpone the runoff and the general election.
>
> I got the impression Giuliani wanted to buy time to figure out all the legal complexities of changing the law. The impression I got was that Giuliani needed more time to manipulate the state legislature, so he could find a way to run for a third term. My doing this would have sent a sort of message to Pataki, giving him some sort of bipartisan cover.
>
> After thinking about it for two hours, I

> told Lhota I would not do it. I wouldn't let
> myself be used for this, even though I opposed
> term limits on principle.

Giuliani kept working the phones, discussing different strategies on how to remain in office. He talked to some people about just remaining an extra ninety days, about an "extended transition." At the same time, he talked to state legislative leaders about the possibility of remaining four more years through an outright repeal of term limits. Assembly Speaker Silver told the *Post* that Giuliani told him directly he wanted a third term.

Giuliani's advisers told the city's power brokers that only Giuliani could hold the city together in this time of peril. They made the argument that the two leading Democrats—Fernando Ferrer and Mark Green—were antagonistic to the police, and this would complicate the transition, and the governing of the city.

On September 25, Michael Bloomberg won the Republican nomination. Fernando Ferrer finished first in the Democratic primary and would face runner-up Mark Green in an October 11 runoff election.

The next day, Giuliani decided he would meet with all three finalists seeking to replace him and try to gain their voluntary support for an extra ninety days in power for himself.

He also decided he would keep lobbying in private, at the same time, for the repeal of term limits, and four more years in power. It was a two-track strategy.

Bloomberg and Mark Green quickly agreed to give Giuliani the extra ninety days, even though there was no provision in the law for such a deal.

But Fernando Ferrer had his doubts. His gut told him the whole thing was antidemocratic. He did not believe that Giuliani was indispensable to the continuity of government, or the recovery of the city.

At 10:15 P.M. on September 26, Ferrer arrived at the mayor's emergency command center at 54th Street and Twelfth Avenue. Ferrer came with his three closest campaign advisers—Bronx Democratic leader Roberto Ramirez, his former Deputy Borough President Ken Knuckles, and Luis Miranda, who had served in the Koch, Dinkins, and Giuliani administrations. Ferrer did not know what to expect. He had been told Lhota would be in the meeting, and perhaps others, so he brought his closest confidants with him.

"Before I got to the command center," Ferrer told me in an extended interview, "I had a conversation with Mark Green. And Mark led me to believe he was going to reject the deal. But when I got there, I had to wait about ninety minutes for Rudy to get there. And during that waiting period, Joe Lhota told me that Green had already accepted the deal. So I was a little unclear."

While waiting for the meeting to start, Ferrer remembers thinking: "The ninety-day proposition has to be unconstitutional. . . . You can't overthrow term limits for just one person. . . . It was nuts to be scheming like this with downtown in ruins. . . . Why was everyone taking the 90-day offer so seriously?. . . . The ninety-day extension had to be devised to buy Rudy time, so he could get the whole four years. I am ready to serve if I win. I am not an apprentice."

Finally, at about 11:45 P.M., Giuliani arrived and asked Ferrer to meet with him alone. Knuckles and Miranda were asked to wait outside.

Giuliani opened the meeting by telling Ferrer, "I would like your support for the 90-day extension. . . . The business community is skittish. They want me to stay on and restore confidence."

Ferrer then began to ask the mayor a series of questions about how the city would actually be governed during this transition with two elected mayors. How would power be shared in practice?

"Who would draft the preliminary budget for the next year?" Ferrer asked.

"Me," Giuliani replied.

"Is this extension only for you, and nobody else?"

"It's just for me."

"This has implications for the Voting Rights Act," Ferrer pointed out. "Have you checked with the Justice Department?"

"Yes," the mayor replied.

"Are you confident you can get pre-clearance from Justice?" Ferrer said, pressing for explicit clarity.

"Haven't you noticed," Giuliani retorted. "This is a different Justice Department."

Giuliani then dangled both the stick and the carrot before Ferrer, who had grown up in poverty in the South Bronx, shining shoes on Fox Street.

"I will have to convince the people who want me to stay four more years to let me settle for just three months," Giuliani said. The mayor claimed that 65 percent of the people wanted him to stay four more years.

"If I accept this deal," Ferrer shot back, "I would have to convince *my* supporters, who want you out *now*."

As the meeting ended, Ferrer promised to give Giuliani's proposal "thoughtful consideration," and give him an answer the next day.

After the meeting broke up, Ferrer noticed a revealing Giuliani moment, an "*Invisible Man*" moment about race.

Giuliani embraced Ramirez and Miranda, Ferrer's two Latino advisers who were waiting outside.

Then Ferrer began to introduce Giuliani to his black friend, Ken Knuckles, who was both a lawyer and an architect; a member of the City Planning Commission, a vice president of Columbia University, and the city's Commissioner of General Services under Dinkins.

In the middle of the introduction, Giuliani wheeled around and walked away, refusing to recognize Knuckles's existence. They had been standing two feet apart.

Ferrer then drove home to the Bronx, thinking he was "95 percent" convinced he would reject the offer.

The next morning at his campaign headquarters, Ferrer was deluged with phone calls urging him to accept the deal.

Richard Grasso, the president of the New York Stock Exchange, called and pleaded with him to give Giuliani the three extra months. His own biggest campaign contributor urged him to say yes. His campaign staff was split 50–50.

At about noon, Green called and told Ferrer he was putting out a statement endorsing the three-month extension for Giuliani.

A half hour later, Ferrer issued his own statement, saying he had rejected the deal.

Ferrer's "No, in Thunder," galvanized the resistance to Giuliani's power grab that had been dormant during the private maneuvering.

The next day (September 28) the *New York Times* published a ringing editorial under the headline THE MAYOR'S DANGEROUS IDEA. The editorial began:

> This is a terrible idea. Neither New York City nor the nation has ever postponed the transfer of power because the public was convinced it could not get along without the current incumbent. The very concept goes against the most basic American convictions, that we live in a nation governed by the rules of law.
>
> To suggest the city would be incapable of getting along without Mr. Giuliani after the end of the year undermines New York's sense of self-sufficiency and normality, which the mayor himself had worked so hard to restore.

The editorial continued:

> While Mr. Giuliani has been a great leader during this crisis, the truth is that no one is indis-

pensable. George Washington understood that when
he rejected repeated attempts to keep him in
office indefinitely. Washington was followed in
the presidency by a long line of successors,
some of them distinctly mediocre. But the
country went on, because the people put their
faith in the democratic process, and not in the
strength of one individual.

That same day, the *Daily News* published the results of an on-line poll that asked the question: "Should the Mayoral candidates agree to let Mayor Giuliani stay in office beyond his term?"

The result showed that 55 percent said no, and 45 percent said yes. The question drew 8,340 responses.

The result directly contradicted Giuliani's contention that 65 percent of the city wanted him to remain in power—a statistic he also shared with Bloomberg and Green, as well as Ferrer. The mayor's staff leaked this fictional 65 percent figure to reporters, in hopes of feeding the bandwagon psychology.

The combination of Ferrer's defiant, contrarian democratic stand, the *Times* editorial, and the results of the *News* poll, began to suck the momentum out of the Giuliani Forever movement. This resistance dissolved nostalgia, sentimentality, and the illusion of inevitability.

On September 29, Giuliani made a direct public appeal, at his daily press briefing, for more time in office, arguing a prolonged transition was necessary because of the terrorist attack.

"All I care about is the future of the city," he said. "There is no other motivation, no other desire."

Four days later, the Giuliani Forever movement officially collapsed. It could not budge the Democratic majority in the state assembly.

What happened was that virtually every member of the assembly's Black and Puerto Rican Caucus, whom Giuliani had shunned for years, told Silver he must block this power grab, that his own job as Speaker could be in jeopardy if he capitulated to Giuliani. A few years earlier, a group of upstate Democrats had attempted a coup to oust Silver. And the black and Puerto Rican assemblymen from the city had supported him at the hour of truth. So now Silver had to repay this debt in the endgame confrontation over control of New York City.

Silver stopped the term-repeal drive adroitly. He announced he would not take up the issue till after the runoff for mayor. This placed it after the legal deadline to give Giuliani the Conservative Party ballot line. Silver used parliamentary timing to checkmate Giuliani.

Now, looking back, this power grab seems like a hallucination during a high fever. It was illegal, antidemocratic, unprecedented, and supremely selfish. But it came within a hair of happening. Powerful corporate, real estate, media, and political forces had bought into the hallucination. Bloomberg and Green had ratified it with their acceptances. Influential leaders, who invoked the rule of law as a habit, were suddenly willing to bend the rule of law. Giuliani's folk-hero halo made a portion of the permanent government act like groupies.

The majority of New Yorkers seemed to feel an emotional paradox. They were grateful to Giuliani, and admiring of his leadership under pressure, but they did not necessarily want to suspend the law so Giuliani could put them through four more years of obedience training.

They revered him like a Charles Lindbergh or General Douglas MacArthur, but they did not want to give him more power over them. They perceived him as dazzling—but dispensable.

New Yorkers didn't want a king, who "ain't satisfied till he rules everything."

Giuliani's bid to stay in power beyond his constitutional term has to be seen in the context of all his other attacks on civil liberties, democratic rights, violations of the rule of law, and attempts to usurp power from individuals and private institutions. He tried to censor art, silence critics, and use the power of government to punish groups and individuals he did not like.

Giuliani illegally released the sealed juvenile-arrest record of Patrick Dorismond without a court order, after he was killed by the police.

He tried to censor works of art at the Brooklyn Museum that offended him, by illegally withholding public funds. He de-funded the Coalition for the Homeless when they disagreed with his policies.

He abused his power by illegally preventing groups he

disapproved of from holding peaceful rallies on the public steps of City Hall, while allowing groups he approved of, like the Yankees, to use those same public steps for rallies.

His police department illegally stopped and frisked minorities without probable cause.

He tried to suppress an advertisement satirizing him.

The courts ruled that Giuliani had violated First Amendment freedoms in twenty-seven different cases.

Giuliani's attempt to repeal term limits just for himself stands in the context of this pattern of arrogating, usurping, and abusing power.

In an unpublished essay, NYCLU senior staff lawyer Art Eisenberg placed the campaign to stay in power within this unconstitutional framework. Eisenberg wrote:

> Mr. Giuliani's efforts violated two constitutional principles. The first principle holds that, as a matter of *due process*, we do not change the rules of an election in the middle of a contest, and the electoral contest for Mayor had begun prior to September 11.
>
> Second, constitutional protections of *equal protection* demand government neutrality in the administration of elections, and prohibit the adoption of rules designed to advantage or promote a particular office seeker.
>
> Fortunately, Mr. Giuliani ultimately abandoned the unseemly efforts to extend his tenure in office. But the fact he could seriously

entertain such efforts demonstrated the weak-
ness of his commitment to the rule of law, and
to even-handed democratic process.

It demonstrated his utter failure to appreciate that the peaceful transition of government represents the hallmark of American
democracy.

In all of American history, there is no precedent can-
celing a democratic transition because of a crisis.

George Washington refused to remain in office as the
nation's first president, at a time of great uncertainty and
fragility. He insisted that there be an election to choose
the second president.

Abraham Lincoln did not try to cancel the election of
1864, even though the nation was in the middle of a Civil
War, to restore the union, end slavery, and rededicate
America to its founding documents.

Franklin Roosevelt did not cancel the election of 1944,
even though the nation was in the middle of the Second
World War, to defeat a genocidal fascism and preserve
democracy.

If Washington, Lincoln, and FDR were not indispensable, than neither was Rudy Giuliani.

8.
Summing Up

At age fifty-eight, Rudy Giuliani still believes he has a chance to become president.

This has been his ambition ever since he saw Jack Kennedy get elected in 1960, breaking the barrier of prejudice that had locked Catholics out of the White House since the birth of the republic.

Giuliani now transcends conventional party politics, with a national approval rating of more than 80 percent. His entrance upon any stage now ignites an ovation. He gets paid $100,000 per speech. He offers patriotic chicken soup. And the audience swoons, thinking they have just heard Abraham Lincoln.

This is what mania is.

It's like the Beatlemania of 1964, when teenage girls couldn't hear the words sung by the Beatles because they were screaming so loud, but some of them fainted anyway from the mass hysteria.

Giuliani now has to milk this mania until he can figure out when, and how, to reenter politics. He already tells interviewers that he wants to return to public office.

One option Giuliani is considering is to wait and run directly for president in 2008. But it will be difficult to sustain his present standing, which one of his advisers has called the political equivalent of God. But memory fades, and icons rust.

Giuliani could possibly run for governor of New York in 2006, when he will be sixty-two. Or, less plausibly, he could challenge Hillary Clinton for New York's Senate seat that same year.

Some of Giuliani's friends cling to the hope that President Bush might turn to him as his vice presidential running mate in 2004, if, for any reason, Dick Cheney is not asked to run again.

But this seems to be wishful thinking. It's hard to imagine Giuliani as a subordinate team player. And Giuliani's liberalish views on choice, gun control, and gay rights would antagonize the fundamentalist Christian Right, which is central to Bush's coalition. It seems that if Bush trusted Giuliani, or wanted to get to know him better, he might have appointed him to be in charge of the new Homeland Security Agency, but he chose Tom Ridge instead.

Other Giuliani allies dream of his running again for mayor of New York in 2005. But this also seems like a long shot.

Mayor Bloomberg has been deferential to Giuliani, and careful never to criticize him directly. But in his own understated way, Bloomberg has changed many of Giuliani's policies, and has become popular doing so.

Bloomberg quietly dropped Giuliani's costly and disruptive plans for a new Yankee Stadium on the West Side of Manhattan.

Bloomberg also resolved a series of lawsuits that Giuliani had stubbornly refused to settle, with groups he did not care for.

In September 2002, Bloomberg agreed to pay millions of dollars in fines—dating back to 1995—to thousands of homeless families who were forced to stay overnight in a Bronx intake office, in unsanitary and unhealthy conditions, with their young children.

For years the Giuliani administration stalled a settlement by arguing that some of the payments to the homeless families had to be in the form of services, not cash. A judge had ruled in a 1995 consent decree that these families, who had sought emergency housing, were entitled to $150 for each night they slept on the floor in the Bronx intake office. The Bloomberg administration agreed to resolve the issue with cash payments.

Bloomberg settled another long-festering lawsuit over the city's community gardens that preserved 500 of them. Giuliani had wanted to sell these open green spaces to the highest bidders for development. The resolution included a compromise that allowed some of the gardens to be converted into housing. Giuliani had kept the dispute in the courts for years.

Bloomberg also adopted somewhat kinder and gentler policies towards the homeless and welfare recipients—while still using Giuliani's vocabulary about a culture of dependency.

Bloomberg approved Ray Kelly's two major reforms that helped improve police/community relations—the end of racial profiling by the NYPD, and the disbanding of the Street Crime Unit, whose members killed Amadou Diallo.

A *New York Magazine* article in September 2002 described Giuliani as "extremely critical," in private, of the elimination of the Street Crime Unit. Giuliani identified with this unit's street aggression, and defended it vigorously when there was widespread criticism after the Diallo shooting.

Bloomberg's police reforms, and his less-confrontational personality, have contributed to better race relations in the city. A June 2002 *New York Times* poll showed that, *for the first time in 14 years,* a majority of respondents *of all races* said racial relations were generally good. The poll found that 53 percent of blacks, 56 percent of Hispanics, and 69 percent of whites thought race relations are good.

In contrast, when Giuliani was mayor two years earlier, only 16 percent of blacks felt race relations in the city were good.

And under Bloomberg and Kelly—a vastly superior police commissioner to Safir—crime has continued to go down, despite the slumping economy, higher unemployment, and increasing homelessness. As of November 1, 2002, major crimes were down almost 5 percent compared to 2001. The murder rate was down 10 percent. New York was on track to have fewer than 600 homicides for the first time in forty years, while Los Angeles and Chicago were suffering dramatic increases in their murder rates.

So, not too surprisingly, a poll taken in July 2002 showed that while Giuliani was enjoying his 80 percent approval rating nationally, Bloomberg was tied with him when matched in a hypothetical duel for mayor of New York.

Politically, Giuliani is a comet trapped in a holding pattern, a jetliner without an airport. While he makes his fortune at Giuliani Partners, he has to wait for a public office to open up. His national celebrity is astonishing, but Giuliani has no clear path back to power.

The essential purpose of this book is to raise questions about Giuliani's qualifications for national leadership and a return to power, based on an exploration of his full record as mayor.

I have tried to honor what Giuliani did on his best day, but not neglect what he did on all his other days. I respect his intelligence, tenacity, and decisiveness. I admire the reductions in crime, and the improvements in the quality of life, that his appointees accomplished. But even here, he hogged the glory, forced out Bill Bratton as the commissioner, and wouldn't promote top Bratton aides, John Timoney or Jack Maple—both men of exceptional talent.

His immense strengths are counterbalanced by immense weaknesses of temperament, opportunism, and intolerance. *His dark side is very dark. His downside is very deep.*

One of the most chilling descriptions of this dark side comes from Rudy Crew, his schools chancellor for four

years, and his intimate friend for three of those years.
Crew really knew Giuliani. They would attend ball games
together, exchange presents, confide their personal problems to each other, and smoke cigars and sip wine
together on the porch of Gracie Mansion. Then they fell
out when Giuliani changed his position and suddenly
wanted to fund school vouchers, after years of under-
funding the schools.

Crew gave Kevin Keating an unusually frank three-
hour interview for Keating's now-completed documentary
film on Giuliani. This is what Crew told Keating:

> There is something deeply pathological about
> Rudy's humanity. It's self-serving. He's built
> his intelligence around survival. And every
> human relationship is one to be survived for
> him, not to be enjoyed.
>
> It became clear to me when I would talk to
> Rudy about race, that he was *barren*-completely
> emotionally *barren* on the issue of race. He
> couldn't see or hear anything other than his
> own political career. . . . He doesn't let the
> possibility of anything other than his own will
> prevailing. . . . He is so incredibly self-cen-
> tered that no one else's feelings are even part
> of the radar screen. . . . He's gotta subjugate
> someone else in order for the relationship to
> work. . . .
>
> For lots of other people there is family,

friends, extended family. He crosses none of
those bridges. He builds none of these outer
circles. That's just who he is. . . . On Monday
he could be my friend, and on Tuesday, he
could tell them to fire me, and then say,
"Don't take it personally . . ."

It's just outside the range of what I think
of as personal decency.

It's outside the range of his self, that
you would start to think-how would I understand other people? How would I understand
their history? How would I come to understand
their culture?

He can't transact any business in that,
because he's never understood any of that. . . .

It's tragic how wounded this man really is.
And wounded people inevitably wound other
people.

Crew's remarks are a survivor's account of a prolonged
encounter with Giuliani. By itself, they might be partially
discounted as sour grapes.

But many other political players see Giuliani's essential
character the same way.

Reverend Floyd Flake, the former Queens congressman
who campaigned in black neighborhoods for Giuliani's
re-election in 1997, told Giuliani to his face, after the 1999
Diallo killing, "You've got a mean streak in you."

Later Flake said, "Anyone who disagrees with him is

treated almost as a personal enemy. He treats everything as if it's a urinating contest."

Mary Brosnahan Sullivan, the director of the Coalition for the Homeless, told me:

I felt sort of seduced and abandoned by Giuliani. We tutored him on the homeless issue in
1989, and briefed him again in 1993. I thought
he was sincere. Then he turned against the
most vulnerable people in society on a dime.
It was so cold and calculating. He suddenly
saw the homeless as his Willie Horton issue
late in the 1993 campaign, and overnight he
went against the homeless without even telling
us. One day he suddenly challenged the right
to shelter.

The problem with Giuliani is that to a
hammer, everything looks like a nail. And to
a prosecutor like him, every homeless person
looks like a criminal.

I thought he was sincere in 1989 when he
visited shelters, and promised a system of
smaller, more humane shelters. When he turned
on us in 1993, I thought it was ruthless
opportunism. But after he was elected mayor,
his attitude hardened into something even
worse-into hatred. He despised the poor after
a while.

Basil Paterson has a slightly different take on how Giuliani's mind works, and on what motivates his behavior.

Paterson was deputy mayor under Ed Koch in the 1970s, was the chairman of the judicial screening panels for both Koch and Mario Cuomo, and is now the labor lawyer representing four municipal unions with a combined membership of 175,000 city employees.

Interviewed in September 2002, Paterson told me:

```
I think Giuliani has a devil in him. He should
have gone to a priest and had an exorcism per-
formed on himself.

    The man is too intelligent to do some of
the things he has done. I can't think of any
other explanation except a devil theory. There
is an evil spirit inside this SOB. Why else
would he do so many things that are vicious
and self-defeating? Why else would he attack
so many different groups-blacks, Latinos,
unions, poor people, artists, taxi drivers,
the homeless? It was crazy.
```

There is no one psychological, or sociological, or political-science theory that can explain someone as protean as Rudy Giuliani.

But one element is his opportunism, his absence of any core beliefs—except in himself as a man of destiny. Everything is subordinate to his own ambition. He can endorse the liberal Democrat Mario Cuomo for governor, and then—in a flash—trash all the ideas that Cuomo represented.

If scapegoating blacks, or the homeless, or schoolteachers is utilitarian at a particular moment, he will do it with gusto.

Giuliani has proven he will advocate any side of any issue, depending what serves his ambition: school vouchers, the right to shelter, term limits, the First Amendment.

He has changed his political-party registration twice to get jobs he wanted, to advance his career.

But I also think there is an existential truth to the demon theory. There is an irrational devil in Giuliani's psyche that contributed to his policy failures in race relations, public education, individual and artistic freedom, police abuses, and treatment of the poor and the homeless.

There is a deep-seated anger inside Giuliani. Here is a capacity for ice-cold betrayal—as in the cases of Rudy Crew, Bill Bratton, Mary Brosnahan Sullivan, and Reverend Floyd Flake.

There is a compulsion to bully the vulnerable. There is an intolerance for ideas other than his own. And there is a blindness to injustice against black people.

These are personal flaws that can erupt at any time. These eruptions have been strong enough to distort Giuliani's judgment and policy making. They have sometimes subverted his better instincts.

Rudy Giuliani's dark side remains very dark. His downside remains very deep. Perhaps bottomless.

This is the full Rudy that America needs to know.

Acknowledgments

First, I wish to thank my former collaborator Wayne Barrett. He delivered about sixty files and folders to my home when I began this book. They contained valuable research material that Wayne had collected while preparing his own splendid book on Giuliani.

I also owe a debt to the fine reporting in Andrew Kirtzman's biography of Giuliani. I have repeated several telling anecdotes with appropriate credit.

This book grew out of an essay I published in the June 17, 2001 issue of *The Nation* magazine. Among those I interviewed for that article and this book are: Mario Cuomo, Fernando Ferrer, Art Eisenberg of the NYCLU, Mary Brosnahan Sullivan of the Coalition for the Homeless, Patrick Markee, also from the Coalition, Congressman Peter King, New York City Comptroller William Thompson, State Comptroller Carl McCall, Police Commissioner Ray Kelly, Reverend Al Sharpton, Bill Cunningham, Lewis Steel, Basil Paterson, Barry Scheck, Stan Michels, and Richard Emery.

I also interviewed several former members of Giuliani's

administration who fervently desire to remain unidentified by name. As one of them said to me, "Rudy is now the equivalent of God in American politics. I can't afford him even doubting my loyalty to him."

I also watched a rough cut of a documentary film about Giuliani being made by Kevin Keating, who also generously allowed me to read the transcripts of several interviews he conducted.

Art Eisenberg of the NYCLU gave me a copy of his unpublished essay on Giuliani and civil liberties that gave me insights and made important connections for me.

I am blessed that some of my close friends are also students of the Giuliani mayorality. Over the years I have had debates and conversations with some of these whose intellect and information helped shape and reshape my thinking. Among the most instructive have been Jimmy Breslin, Pete Hamill, Nick Pileggi, Kevin McCabe, Milton Mollen, Joe Spinelli, Victor Navasky, Wayne Barrett, Bill Lynch, Ken Knuckles, Dennis Rivera, Ken Sunshine, Tom Puccio, and three people no longer with us: Eric Breindel, Jack Maple, and Murray Kempton.

They all had different points of view, and none are responsible for the judgments I reached.

Most of all, this book is informed by my own intensive reporting on Giuliani, starting twenty years ago. I have also made use of a series of private dinners I enjoyed with Giuliani, where I got to know at least part of the private man.

These sporadic, and always pleasant evenings took place between 1983 and 1999.

My editor, Carl Bromley, made this a pleasant project with his surgical pencil, historical perspective, and literary wit. His assistant, Ruth Baldwin, lent her precision, efficiency, and sunny disposition to the editing and production process.

—Jack Newfield

About the Author

Jack Newfield is a prize-winning investigative journalist and documentary filmmaker who has written eight previous books. From 1964 to 1988 Newfield was a writer for the *Village Voice* in New York City. He then wrote a column for the *New York Daily News* and resigned during the 1990 strike rather than cross a picket line. He was the only management employee to join the strike. From 1991 to 2001 he was a columnist for the *New York Post*. He is now a fellow at the Nation Institute.

Among his earlier books are: *A Prophetic Minority*, a study of the origins of the student and civil rights movement of the early 1960s; *Robert Kennedy: A Memoir*; *The Permanent Government*, an expose of the power elite of New York City; *Only in America: The Life and Crimes of Don King*; and his memoir of last year, *Somebody's Got to Tell It*.

Newfield won the 1980 George Polk award for his muck-raking the worst judges and landlords of New York City series in the *Village Voice* and an Emmy Award for writing and reporting the PBS Frontline documentary *Don King: Unauthorized*.

He lives in New York City with his wife of thirty-one years, Janie Eisenberg, a therapist.